W9-BFG-742

Research Methods Laboratory Manual for Psychology

William Langston

Middle Tennessee State University

WADSWORTH

THOMSON LEARNING

Australia • Canada • Mexico • Singapore • Spain • United Kingdom • United States

WADSWORTH

THOMSON LEARNING

Sponsoring Editor: *Vicki Knight*
Marketing Manager: *Joanne Terhaar*
Editorial Assistants: *Julie Dillemuth,*
    Dan Moneypenny
Production Editor: *Kirk Bomont*
Production Service: *Scratchgravel Publishing*
    Services
Manuscript Editor: *Margaret Pinette*

Permissions Editor: *Sue Ewing*
Interior Design: *Anne Draus*
Cover Design: *Vernon Boes, Roy Neuhaus*
Cover Photo: *J. A. Kraulis/Masterfile*
Interior Illustration: *Greg Draus*
Print Buyer: *Vena Dyer*
Typesetting: *Scratchgravel Publishing Services*
Printing and Binding: *Webcom*

For more information about this or any other Wadsworth products, contact:
WADSWORTH
511 Forest Lodge Road
Pacific Grove, CA 93950 USA
www.wadsworth.com
1-800-423-0563 (Thomson Learning Academic Resource Center)

For permission to use material from this work, contact us by
Web: www.thomsonrights.com
Fax: 1-800-730-2215
Phone: 1-800-730-2214

Printed in Canada

10   9   8   7   6   5   4   3   2

Library of Congress Cataloging-in-Publication Data

Langston, William, [date]–
    Research methods laboratory manual for psychology / William Langston.
        p.   cm.
    Includes bibliographical references and index.
    ISBN 0-534-55683-3 (alk. paper)
        1. Psychology—Research—Methodology.   I. Title.

    BF76.5 .L36 2001
    150'.7'24—dc21

                                                    2001026020

To William Epstein,
whose target article approach to teaching research
methods inspired this manual and who may
recognize some of the target articles inside

About the Author

William Langston is an assistant professor of psychology at Middle Tennessee State University. He has a bachelor's degree in psychology from the University of Houston and a Ph.D. in psychology from the University of Wisconsin–Madison. His graduate minor was in computer science. His teaching interests include research methods, cognitive psychology, and the psychology of language.

Langston has published papers in a number of research journals in the areas of memory and language. He is a member of the Psychonomic Society, APA Division Two—Teaching of Psychology, the Society for Text and Discourse, and the Cognitive Science Society. He has twice served on the committee hosting the Middle Tennessee Psychological Association student research conference, once as its chair.

Outside of work, Langston spends time refining his stand-up routine and writing unpublished fiction.

Brief Contents

Contents

■ ■ ■ ■ ■ ■

PART TWO

Experimental Designs — 37

Preface

I wrote this manual to fill a need. There are plenty of textbooks for research methods classes. However, there are few options for the laboratory. In my experience, students work at least as hard on their independent research in the laboratory as they work in the course. This manual is designed to help them do that.

Features for Students

The exciting features for students are:

1. Each chapter is based on a target article that is a very good example of how the methodology in that chapter should be used. Students get to learn by seeing how some of the top people in the field have addressed similar questions.
2. The projects are educational. Several of the projects in the manual have been presented by students at regional and national conferences, including the meetings of the Middle Tennessee Psychological Association and the meetings of the Midwestern Psychological Association.
3. There is a mix of project types. Students can conduct research in the laboratory or in the real world, using computers, paper-and-pencil materials, or observation sheets.
4. Most of what a student needs to conduct research is here in the manual. Students can focus more of their attention on asking (and answering) interesting questions and less on tracking down materials.

Features for Instructors

Exciting features for instructors include:

1. All of the "big" design types for psychology research have been included (observation designs, surveys, and experiments). Instructors don't have to restrict their laboratory projects to experimental designs

2. Many of the content areas in psychology have been sampled for projects (social psychology, personality, clinical psychology, cognition, health psychology, and perception). Students don't have to be future cognitive psychologists to find a project that interests them in this manual.

3. The appendixes cover getting approval for projects from institutional review boards, setting up the data for analysis, writing results sections, and presenting research. These topics present major roadblocks for research projects; the manual is designed to walk students through each step.

4. Even though the manual offers a variety of potential projects, there is a common core that reduces the burden of supervising several totally unrelated projects simultaneously. Instructors can branch out from the areas they know best without tackling a major research project of their own.

5. Because of the variety of designs, students can rehearse their knowledge of all of the analyses covered in introductory statistics (from chi-square to factorial ANOVA).

6. Ethics notes remind students of the ethical rules and highlight situations where those rules may affect how research is conducted. Methodology notes highlight features of target articles and the methodological issues associated with the projects.

7. For the experiments conducted using the software, the data files will be prepared for import into any statistics package. Students can use my software and still analyze their data using a package with which they are already familiar.

For Both Instructors and Students

I chose most of the topics for the chapters from projects conducted by my students (some of their names are in the "acknowledgments" section after this preface). I picked topics that students enjoyed, that would lend themselves to research within the constraints of the class, and that left plenty of unanswered questions for students to work on. I also picked topics that interested me personally.

You can use this manual in one of two ways. If you have a methodology in mind (as in, "I want to do a survey"), turn to the chapter covering that methodology. If you can choose any methodology, pick a topic that you like. If none of my project ideas interest you, the materials are generally flexible enough to let you strike out on your own. Here are some additional suggestions for how to use this manual:

1. The organization is the same for each chapter. A basic methodology is introduced, a target article that used that methodology is described, and projects are suggested. Some of the users of this book will need to pick a project topic early in the course, probably before any of the methodologies have been described. If that's the case for you, start by choosing a topic that you like, then read the entire chapter related to that topic. The opening section should tell you enough about the method to help you understand the target article, and that should help you decide if the topic is really

right for you. If you have already read about a methodology before choosing a topic, skip the opening section. Your instructor and your textbook will already have prepared you to understand the target article (of course, it can never hurt to go over the basics one more time).

2. A lot of projects are suggested for each target article. Some of these are directly related to the experiments in the target article; some are more distantly related. Most of them have been tried by students in my classes. I will tell you up front that not all of the projects will "work." Some of the ideas go beyond the safe area where we know what the results will be. That is what makes them interesting. If you are concerned about conducting a project that does not provide the result you expect, stick to the first couple of suggestions. If you are feeling brave, go farther down the list. To help you choose, the projects are rated for difficulty, as indicated by the presence of one, two, or three stars (with one star being the easiest). I tried to evaluate the following when rating the projects: amount of work gathering materials, amount of work conducting the research, possibilities for profound experimenter error, likelihood of an outcome that makes the experimenter unhappy, and the complexity of the literature. One-star projects will be low on some or all of these dimensions; three-star projects will be high on some or all of these dimensions. Choose the level of difficulty that is right for you.

3. The suggested projects are in no way intended to limit what you do. Most of my students create projects that are similar to some of the suggestions but are not specifically like any one of them. The risks are higher if you do this, and you will work a little harder, but there is the potential to uncover a new fact about psychology.

4. Keep in mind that there are a lot of research materials in the manual. If you come up with a project from Chapter 2 that involves assessing the mood of your participants, the Brief Mood Introspection Scale discussed in Chapter 7 may be useful to you. Be sure to look at the other chapters for materials for your project.

Happy researching. Let me know about the projects you try and how they come out.

■ ■ ■ ■ ■ ■
Acknowledgments

Thanks to all of the students who have tested the projects that appear in the manual. Thanks also to Neil Norman for assisting me with the Windows versions of the software. Also, thank you to the reviewers whose careful reading and valuable suggestions have greatly improved the quality of this manual: Steven Horowitz, Central Connecticut State University; Mary Jo Litten, Pittsburgh State University; James Sutterer, Syracuse University; Aurora Torres, University of Alabama; and Lynn White, Southern Utah University. I can't say that the review process has been the best chapter of my life; however, the final version of this manual is much better due to the reviewers' efforts.

I would like to extend a special thank you to Vicki Knight, my editor at Wadsworth. Her patience and dedication to this project have vastly improved the quality of the finished product. I would also like to acknowledge the incredible production team who made the finished book what it is. I was lucky to have the services of the team at Scratchgravel Publishing Services (Anne, Greg, and Elizabeth Draus). They made the process painless. Kirk Bomont coordinated production, and I especially appreciate his help when problems arose with Chapter 8. I would also like to thank Margaret Pinette for copy editing, Sue Ewing for assistance with permissions, and Joanne Terhaar for her work in marketing.

Justin Barrett, Brandi Cirotto, and Michal Moseley (Middle Tennessee State University) conducted the bar observation described in project 3d (Chapter 1) for their research methods lab project. Their study was presented at the spring meeting of the Middle Tennessee Psychological Association in May 1999.

Kristin Cather, Becky Short, and Laura Bailey (Middle Tennessee State University) investigated the relationship between pet ownership and stress (Chapter 3) for their research methods lab project. This study was presented at the spring meeting of the Middle Tennessee Psychological Association in May 1998.

Thanks to Stuart Bernstein (Middle Tennessee State University) for helping to pilot test the software (Chapter 4) in his research methods classes.

The caffeine experiment discussed in project 3 (Chapter 4) was conducted by Billy Bruce, Rebekah Stephens, and Beth Bolton at Middle Tennessee State University as their laboratory project in the fall 1999 semester.

Tara Appleton and Mindy Patterson (Middle Tennessee State University) developed the design in project 2a (Chapter 5) for their research methods lab project. Their study was presented at the spring meeting of the Middle Tennessee Psychological Association in May 1999.

Chad Hughes and Dawn Little (Middle Tennessee State University) developed the design in project 2c1 (Chapter 5) for their research methods lab project. Their study was presented at the spring meeting of the Middle Tennessee Psychological Association in April 2000.

Laura Eilar, Jenni Farrow, Julianne Sim, and J. Christopher Staub (Denison University) developed the design in project 6a (Chapter 5) for an explorations in cognitive science lab project.

Tracey Fox, Patti Howard, and Neil Norman (Middle Tennessee State University) conducted the Stroop experiment described in project 2d (Chapter 6) for their research methods lab project. Their study won the outstanding research prize for experimental psychology at the MTSU Psychology Day in November 1998. The text of their poster was used for the sample poster in Appendix D.

Project 3b (Chapter 6) was suggested by a reviewer.

Sarah Frazier, Janet Herrod, and Charles Webster (Middle Tennessee State University) designed the story continuation experiment described in project 3c (Chapter 7) for their research methods lab project. Their study was presented at the spring meeting of the Middle Tennessee Psychological Association in May 1999.

Thanks to Morton Gernsbacher for providing the sentences from the Foertsch and Gernsbacher (1997) experiments.

The project described in 2e (Chapter 8) was developed as a class project in the psychology of language laboratory course at Denison University in the fall of 1996. Coral Keith, Voloe Scott, and Matthew Springer also helped prepare the presentation of the results. This experiment was presented at the Midwestern Psychological Association meeting in May 1997.

The target article for Chapter 9 was suggested by John Pennington (Middle Tennessee State University). His students originally developed the designs in projects 2a (Jeffrey Thomas, Heidi Welch, Jessica Ray, and Valerie Sweatt) and 2b (Maile Porter, Kari Thoman, Hunter Jones, and Kerri Mills) for their research methods lab projects. Both studies were presented at the spring meeting of the Middle Tennessee Psychological Association in May 1999.

The target article for Chapter 10 was originally used to illustrate strong inference by William Epstein at the University of Wisconsin–Madison in his research methods course. In preparing this chapter, I consulted notes I made as his teaching assistant in 1993.

The target articles for Chapter 11 were originally used to illustrate the relationship between correlation studies and experiments by William Epstein at the University of Wisconsin–Madison in his research methods course. In preparing this chapter, I consulted notes I made in 1993 as his teaching assistant.

Eric Gauen and George Carlson (Middle Tennessee State University) conducted the experiment described in project 3 (Chapter 11) for their research methods lab project. Their study was presented at the spring meeting of the Middle Tennessee Psychological Association in April 2000.

Jennifer Gress (Denison University) included judged control as a dependent variable in an honors project examining the effects of environmental crowding (Chapter 11).

In Appendix D, the speaker presenting facts that were false was James Kalat, and the speaker presenting the memory demonstration was James Nairne. I saw both of these speakers at the meetings of the Middle Tennessee Psychological Association. A lot of the tips on making an oral presentation came from my experience as a graduate student in Arthur Glenberg's laboratory.

Thanks also to the faculty at the University of Wisconsin–Madison, who instilled in me a love of methodology to go with my love of psychology, and to the faculty at Middle Tennessee State University, who have put up with me talking about this manual for the past three years. Finally, thanks to my family for making it all possible.

William Langston

Part One

Naturalistic Observation, Survey, and Correlation Research

The research techniques in Part One all involve measuring behavior or opinions without manipulating anything. With naturalistic observation, the researcher observes what happens without intervening. With survey research, the researcher asks questions of participants. Correlation research is used to find relationships using naturalistic observation or survey techniques.

Naturalistic Observation

Protecting your parking space

People exhibit territoriality when confronted with intruders, even in public spaces. Will people exhibit territorial behavior when the thing they are defending has no value? The topic of the research discussed here is parking spaces. When a person is ready to leave a parking space, controlling the space no longer offers any benefit, and lingering in the space is a waste of time. This chapter summarizes research by Ruback and Juieng (1997) that shows that, nonetheless, people do exhibit territorial behavior (they leave more slowly) when someone is waiting for their parking space.

■ ■ ■ ■ ■ ■
Introduction: Observing Behavior

What makes psychological research so difficult to conduct? Basically, the thing we are trying to study (the human psyche) is not available for direct observation. You cannot open the top of a person's head and peer inside to find out about emotions, motivations, thought processes, or disorders. Instead, we observe behavior and use that to make inferences about the parts that cannot be observed.

The simplest type of behavioral observation is to ask people what they are thinking or why they do what they do. Some psychological research is done using this technique (and we will see how in Chapters 2 and 3). A problem with this approach is that people often do not know why they do what they do or how they do what they do. Sometimes, people know why they do what they do, but social forces make them uncomfortable admitting their true motivation, and so they lie when asked.

When we are concerned that asking people about psychological activity will not yield useful information, we can observe people's behavior and use that to infer their underlying motivations. The simplest way to do this is to use a technique called **naturalistic observation**. Basically, you observe what happens in a situation without the participants knowing that they are being observed.

ETHICS NOTE 1.1   If you have already learned about research ethics, you might wonder how we can observe people without their permission, given that research participants should give informed consent before the research begins. Two factors are usually considered when deciding whether observational research is ethical. The first has to do with whether the observer is in any way involved in the situation. As long as people are acting in a public place and engaging in behaviors they would have engaged in whether the observer was present or not, it is usually considered acceptable to observe them. The second factor has to do with anonymity. Provided that the first concern is satisfied, if there is no way that any individual participant could be identified as having participated, the observation will probably be acceptable. As with any other project, observation research is always checked by an institutional review board (see Appendix A), and these people will decide if the potential risk exceeds the potential value. As long as the risk is low and the value is high, observation research can be conducted ethically.

The observer does not intervene in the situation in any way. If you are a very careful observer of human behavior, and you record all of the events that transpire, you may be able to discover relationships that suggest the operation of underlying psychological variables.

One thing you have to be careful about when collecting observations is that you do not interfere with the situation. When you intervene, you can no longer be sure that the behavior you are observing is the same as the behavior that would normally be present.

Consider this example from an article in *Reader's Digest* (Ecenbarger, 1998). The title was "America's Worst Drivers," and the author went to various cities to see how badly people drive. In Boston, the author investigated people's reactions at a traffic circle by driving around it. The official policy at traffic circles is that incoming cars yield to cars in the circle. As the author described it, the first time around there were no problems, but after two or three laps, "things started happening." The "things" were that people started cutting in and getting hostile. Maybe people in Boston are hostile at traffic circles, but it is hard to separate that from people's hostility toward cars that just circle without turning anywhere. Crossing the line from naturalistic observation to participating in the event can make it difficult to interpret your results.

What can we learn from observation? The main thing is that we can uncover relationships that exist between behaviors and environmental variables. We can make statements like "if this event happens, a person is likely to respond in this way." We *cannot* say that a particular environmental event will cause a particular behavior. To make cause-and-effect statements will require an experiment (using techniques covered in Part Two). We also cannot say for certain that people will have a particular psychological reaction to a particular environmental event. However, based on their behavior, we can infer something about their mental state that led to the behavior.

Why do observation research? There are three big reasons:

1. *To find out if relationships exist.* Observation research requires careful preparation and can be difficult to carry out, but it is simpler in some ways than doing surveys or experiments. Before investing time and resources in a project to find out why people respond in certain ways to certain events, it is always a good idea to find out if a relationship exists to be studied.
2. *Because observation designs are more natural.* Nothing could be less intrusive than naturalistic observation. Researchers use observation techniques to avoid **participant reactivity** (where people act differently because they know they are being observed). This problem might be worse in psychology than in other sciences because the people we observe sometimes make conscious decisions to change their behavior when they are concerned about how they will be perceived by the researcher.
3. *As a check on information collected using other techniques.* Sometimes a researcher will ask people about their behavior in various situations and then observe them in those situations to see if their self-reports match up with reality. Or a researcher will confirm that behavior in the artificial laboratory environment is consistent with behavior in the real world.

Our target article for this chapter used a naturalistic observation design. The researchers were interested in territoriality in public spaces. The basic questions were: Will people exhibit territorial behaviors in public spaces? and What will influence these behaviors?

■■■■■■
Target Article: Observing Territoriality in the Parking Lot

The target article for this chapter is Ruback and Juieng (1997). The premise for the research was this: There is evidence that people "defend" their territory when it has some value. The defense can take many forms, including aggression. A special case of territoriality is defending a public space. By definition, nobody owns a public space, and therefore nobody has a legitimate right to claim it. But people still defend public spaces, usually by occupying them for a longer period of time. For example, Ruback (1987) found that men in library aisles take longer when intruded upon. Ruback, Pape, and Doriot (1989) found that people spend longer on a pay phone when someone is waiting.

The question for the Ruback and Juieng (1997) research was: Will people defend a public space that has no value to them? They chose the parking lot as the test case for this study. The reasoning was this: When people are leaving a parking space, it is actually detrimental for them to linger there. If you are trying to leave, it does not make much sense to stay longer just to exhibit territoriality.

Do people take longer to leave a parking space when someone is waiting? You probably already have an opinion on this. As an exercise, jot down your honest answer to the questions in Table 1.1.

Table 1.1 How Would You Behave in the Following Situations?

Use this scale to fill in each blank with the most appropriate number:

faster			just as fast			more slowly
1	2	3	4	5	6	7

1. If *I* am backing out of a parking space and someone is waiting, I will back out: _____

2. If *I* am backing out of a parking space and someone is waiting and that driver honks the horn at me, I will back out: _____

3. If *someone else* is backing out of a parking space and someone is waiting, the person will back out: _____

4. If *someone else* is backing out of a parking space and someone is waiting and that driver honks the horn, the person will back out: _____

Most people feel that they will back out a little faster when someone is waiting. Without getting too far ahead of the story, Ruback and Juieng (1997) found that people actually take longer to back out of a parking space when someone is waiting. Let's see how they did that (the following discussion is based on their Study 1).

Two hundred drivers were observed in a mall parking lot. For timing, a stopwatch was started when people opened the driver's door, and it was stopped when the front bumper of the car cleared the parking space. The participants did not know that they were being observed. Some drivers were intruded upon by another car waiting for the space (the drivers knew when someone was waiting). The main comparison was between drivers who were intruded upon and drivers who were not.

When another driver was waiting, the average departure time was 39.03 seconds. When nobody was waiting, the average departure time was 32.15 seconds. This difference was significant. In other words, drivers did show territoriality in defending parking spaces. It took about seven seconds longer to back out when someone was waiting. This was the case even though lingering in a parking space is as much a waste of time for the departing driver as it is for the person waiting.

■ ■ ■ ■ ■ ■
Implementing the Design

Materials

For most of the projects below, all you will need is a stopwatch. The supplement to this chapter contains a sample sheet to record your observations for the first project listed below. There are two steps you should take before you begin an observation.

1. Go to the setting where you will be observing, and take notes on what happens. Because you will not know which things will matter in the end, try to

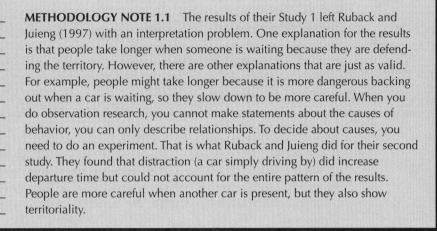

METHODOLOGY NOTE 1.1 The results of their Study 1 left Ruback and Juieng (1997) with an interpretation problem. One explanation for the results is that people take longer when someone is waiting because they are defending the territory. However, there are other explanations that are just as valid. For example, people might take longer because it is more dangerous backing out when a car is waiting, so they slow down to be more careful. When you do observation research, you cannot make statements about the causes of behavior, you can only describe relationships. To decide about causes, you need to do an experiment. That is what Ruback and Juieng did for their second study. They found that distraction (a car simply driving by) did increase departure time but could not account for the entire pattern of the results. People are more careful when another car is present, but they also show territoriality.

write down everything in the situation that might affect behavior. If you plan to use the sample sheet, take it with you, and take notes on anything that is not already on the sheet. A trip to the library may also be useful here. If anyone has already made observations in your setting, his or her ideas can be valuable sources.

2. Use your notes to work out a draft of your observation sheet. You need to make a quick and easy way to record information on all of the things you wrote down in step 1. Then, return to the setting with your sheet and practice recording observations. The goal is to familiarize yourself with the scoring procedure. You can also make changes to your sheet to make it work better in the real world. Observing well can be extremely difficult. Practicing and developing the best recording instrument possible will really help.

Suggested Projects

☆ 1. You can replicate the original Ruback and Juieng (1997) study. Choose a parking lot in a mall, and observe people backing out of spaces. Ruback and Juieng observed spaces near the door, which are more popular and more likely to have people waiting.

2. You could also make minor variations to Ruback and Juieng's (1997) procedure.

☆   a. Some other variables considered by Ruback and Juieng (1997) that have not been discussed so far were the sex of the drivers, the race of the drivers, the number of passengers, and the status of the cars. Your observations could go a bit beyond Ruback and Juieng's by focusing more on these variables.

☆   b. Try a different kind of parking lot situation. People might feel more vulnerable at night. This might increase their flight response and cause them to leave more quickly when someone is waiting. When the lot is really crowded (such as during the holidays) the space may be even

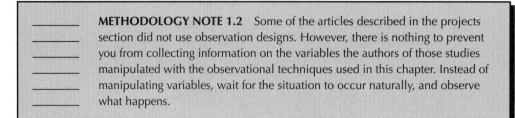

METHODOLOGY NOTE 1.2   Some of the articles described in the projects section did not use observation designs. However, there is nothing to prevent you from collecting information on the variables the authors of those studies manipulated with the observational techniques used in this chapter. Instead of manipulating variables, wait for the situation to occur naturally, and observe what happens.

more valuable, slowing people down more. When people are waiting for "bad" spots (farther from the door), are drivers as territorial as they are with "good" spots?

☆   c. Try a different kind of parking lot. For example, people might be less territorial at church than a mall (based on the different kinds of activity taking place in the two locations).

☆   d. Ruback and Juieng (1997) observed in Atlanta. There may be regional variations in territoriality. Are people as territorial in rural areas? How do people in your part of the country compare to people in Atlanta?

☆☆   e. You could include more variables in your observations. For example, in Study 2 (an experiment that was not discussed above), Ruback and Juieng (1997) manipulated the degree of intrusion and distraction. They had some drivers wait for a space and other drivers honk. To include distraction, they had a driver pass by a parking space as the person was getting in their car. This was an experiment, but you could collect information on these variables using an observation design. Simply record whether or not a car passed by, whether or not the other driver honked, and so on. You could also include additional variables to observe. For example, how do people behave when more than one car is waiting for a spot? How do they behave when a driver actually follows them to their spot?

   3. Observe territoriality in other locations.

☆   a. Ruback and Snow (1993) observed territoriality at a water fountain. Their main variable was the race of the drinkers and intruders. They found that people drank longer when intruded on by someone of a different race.

☆☆   b. Gal, Benedict, and Supinski (1986) looked at territorial markers in the library. Their research involved an experiment and not an observation, but it could be turned into an observational study. They showed people slides of library tables with territorial markers on them (like an open book). They also had different types of tables. They asked people how likely they would be to sit at each table. You could do an observation to see if people's behavior in the library matches what they said to Gal et al. There are two aspects of this: What markers do people use to show that the space is occupied, and how do people act in response to those markers? Do the invaded and the invaders seem to be playing by the same set of rules?

ETHICS NOTE 1.2   Whenever your study involves personal variables (like race), you may encounter difficulty getting approval for your project on ethical grounds. If you have good reason to suspect that personal variables will affect your results, you will be more justified in including them in your study. For example, Ruback and Snow (1993) demonstrated that race is related to territorial behavior in some situations. Ruback and Juieng (1997) included race as one of the variables they recorded. So, you have evidence that race may matter, and you have a precedent for including it in your study. You could make the case that to fully understand the situation in the parking lot, race should be included on your observation sheet. As with other potential ethical issues, if you are motivated by research questions, you will be more likely to receive approval from review boards and more likely to conduct ethical research than if you are proposing "what if" questions.

☆☆   McAndrew, Ryckman, Horr, and Solomon (1978) also did an experiment in the library involving territorial markers. When people left their seats, they moved the people's territorial markers (books, jackets, etc.) and set someone else's stuff up in the spot. Then, they observed people's behavior when they returned. Basically, they found that when someone else's territorial markers were in the person's spot, the territory was surrendered. This suggests several lines of observation. How do people arrange their possessions to keep people out of their spot when they temporarily leave it? Which arrangements really deter intruders? How do intruders "claim" a spot they are invading?

☆☆   c. Werner, Brown, and Damron (1981) investigated territoriality in an arcade. They found that nonutilitarian touching was used as a territorial marker. When intruded upon, players touched the machine to indicate their control over the territory. You could also look at nonutilitarian touching as a territorial marker in arcades or in other settings (such as the check-in counter at a hotel).

☆☆☆   d. Fried and DeFazio (1974) looked at territoriality in subway cars. They found that people preferred the seats that gave them the most physical separation from other passengers. For example, a two-passenger seat is treated as full when only one person is sitting in it until the car is at high passenger density. These seats offer the least opportunity for increasing interpersonal distance when both seats are occupied. One aspect of the subway car that differs from the parking lot is people's degree of exposure. The space in a subway car is basically one big area, and people have no control over it (unlike the privacy of their own car). In these types of public spaces, how do people claim part of the space? For example, how do people mark their area in a crowded bar?

A group of students at Middle Tennessee State University looked at one aspect of territorial marking in a bar. Their question was: Is there any way to protect a table through the use of territorial markers? Out of

35 groups who attempted to hold a table with territorial markers (a drink, package of cigarettes, etc.), 31 lost the table to an intruder. For the 65 groups who attempted to hold a table by leaving one person to guard it, only two tables were lost. It appears that in order to hold on to your space in these situations, you have to stay in it. This still leaves open the question of which cues operate when someone is at a table. Somehow, two groups lost a guarded table. Is there some signal that works better to prevent intrusions?

☆☆☆   e. Barber (1990) investigated home color as a territorial marker. When people's houses were not white, they were less likely to be the same color as their neighbor's house than would have been expected by chance. In other words, people marked their territory by painting their house a different color than that of their neighbors' houses. Sandilands and McMullin (1980) looked at material on faculty members' office doors as a territorial marker. They found that the amount of material was related to status. These studies suggest observing territoriality by looking at more permanent markers on private spaces. How do people mark ownership of their own spaces? What factors seem related to these types of display?

☆☆☆   f. Haber (1980) studied territorial behavior in the classroom. After part of the semester went by and people established which was "their" seat, an invader arrived early and sat in the seat. People's reactions to this invasion were observed. Haber found that people in the center of the room were more likely to defend their territory than people on the periphery (matching with studies of dominance in animals). You could observe behavior in the classroom to see how people mark their seat and how they defend it. You might also consider why people choose a seat and stick with it for a whole semester. Can you observe any differences in territoriality between people who stay in one place and people who move to a new seat each day?

☆☆☆   4. Ruback and Juieng (1997) were looking for a situation where territoriality would reverse. It is not beneficial to wait in a parking space when you are through with it, but people do it anyway. You might try to find a more extreme situation to see if the pattern reverses. For example, it is a good idea to get through a crosswalk as quickly as possible, especially if a car is coming. Will people linger in a crosswalk when a car has to wait for them compared to when no car is waiting?

■ ■ ■ ■ ■ ■
References

Barber, N. (1990). Home color as a territorial marker. *Perceptual and Motor Skills, 71,* 1107–1110.

Ecenbarger, W. (1998). America's worst drivers. *Reader's Digest, 152,* 108–114.

Fried, M. L., & DeFazio, V. J. (1974). Territoriality and boundary conflicts in the subway. *Psychiatry, 37,* 47–59.

Gal, C. A., Benedict, J. O., & Supinski, D. M. (1986). Territoriality and the use of library study tables. *Perceptual and Motor Skills, 63,* 566–574.

Haber, G. M. (1980). Territorial invasion in the classroom: Invadee response. *Environment and Behavior, 12,* 17–31.

McAndrew, F. T., Ryckman, R. M., Horr, W., & Solomon, R. (1978). The effects of invader placement of spatial markers on territorial behavior in a college population. *The Journal of Social Psychology, 104,* 149–150.

Ruback, R. B. (1987). Deserted (and nondeserted) aisles: Territorial intrusion can produce persistence, not flight. *Social Psychology Quarterly, 50,* 270–276.

Ruback, R. B., & Juieng, D. (1997). Territorial defense in parking lots: Retaliation against waiting drivers. *Journal of Applied Social Psychology, 27,* 821–834. Used with permission of the author.

Ruback, R. B., Pape, K., & Doriot, P. D. (1989). Waiting for a phone: Intrusion on callers leads to territorial defense. *Social Psychology Quarterly, 52,* 232–241.

Ruback, R. B., & Snow, J. N. (1993). Territoriality and nonconscious racism at water fountains: Intruders and drinkers (blacks and whites) are affected by race. *Environment and Behavior, 25,* 250–267.

Sandilands, M. L., & McMullin, J. A. (1980). Territorial marking and dominance: A field study in the halls of academia. *Psychological Reports, 46,* 1018.

Werner, C. M., Brown, B. B., & Damron, G. (1981). Territorial marking in a game arcade. *Journal of Personality and Social Psychology, 41,* 1094–1104.

■
■
■
■
■
■
■
■
SUPPLEMENT

Sample Observation Sheet

P#	Start time*	End time†	Waiting‡	Gender	Race	# Passengers	P Car§	I Car‖
			Y / N	M / F				
			Y / N	M / F				
			Y / N	M / F				
			Y / N	M / F				
			Y / N	M / F				
			Y / N	M / F				
			Y / N	M / F				
			Y / N	M / F				
			Y / N	M / F				
			Y / N	M / F				

*Start timing when the driver opens the driver's side door.
†Stop timing when the front bumper clears the parking space.
‡A car is waiting if someone is waiting for the spot *and* the driver turns toward the intruding car before opening his or her car door.
§Participant car. Record model, condition, and approximate age of car.
‖Intruder car. Record model, condition, and approximate age of car.

Survey Research

*This chapter isn't very good,
but I give it an A anyway*

Do students expect higher grades than they ought to? Our target article for this chapter (Landrum, 1999) investigates whether or not students' grade expectations are too high. Students were asked to rate their work in a class and to estimate the grade they deserved. Students' anticipated GPA was higher than the GPA they should have gotten based on their own assessment of the quality of their own work.

■■■■■■ Introduction: Conducting a Survey

How can we find out about the sources of human behavior? One way is to watch people and infer why they do what they do (Chapter 1). Another way is to ask people why they do what they do. That is the topic of this chapter. How are surveys used to understand human behavior?

There are two main uses of surveys. By now, you are familiar with practical uses of surveys. Politicians conduct polls to find out which issues are popular with voters. News organizations conduct polls to find out how people feel about politicians. Businesses conduct polls to find out how people feel about products and services. These results are used for practical purposes. If consumers will not buy an instant bacon product that squeezes out of a tube like toothpaste, nobody will waste time and money manufacturing it.

There are also research applications for surveys. For example, *Consumer Reports* commissioned a survey investigating the effectiveness of psychotherapy (Seligman, 1995; *Consumer Reports*, 1995, November). These data have a practical value to the readers of *Consumer Reports*, but they also serve to demonstrate whether or not psychotherapy is an effective treatment for mental disorders. The results can be used by therapists to optimize their interventions. (As an aside, Seligman's discussion of the methodology of the *Consumer Reports* survey illustrates nicely how to determine if the results of a survey are sound.)

When planning and carrying out a survey, a number of methodological decisions must be made. How researchers handle these issues will have a large impact on the usefulness of their results. Basically, we are trying to get as much information from people as we can without allowing any biases to affect that information. The big issues include:

1. Who will participate in the survey? You start with a **population**. This is a theoretical entity that corresponds to everyone you want to generalize to. Sometimes the population is very large (Nielsen ratings should generalize to the entire country). Sometimes the population is very small (if I want to know whether students in a class would like to postpone an exam, the results should generalize to the class). From this population, you select a **sample**. These are the people you actually survey. You have to be careful to avoid selection biases when choosing a sample. How do you get the sample?

One way is to use **random sampling**. With this technique, every person in the population has an equal chance of being in the sample. It is like throwing all the names in a hat and then drawing them out until you get the number of people you want. For a university population, you could get a random sample by numbering every name in the directory and using a random number table to pick names. If the sample is random, there is a good chance that it will also be **representative**. In other words, its makeup will mirror that of the population. If the sample is representative, you can be confident that the results of your survey will apply to everyone in the population. If your sample is biased, you can only generalize to the people who participated.

Keep in mind that the number of people sampled is usually not the issue, but rather, how they were chosen. Even if 100,000 people visit a news show's Web site and express the same opinion, the results will probably not apply to the population at large. Chances are that only a special subset of the population will vote in a television poll (at the simplest level, only people watching the show will even know that a survey is being conducted). The goal of any survey should be to collect a representative sample from the population of interest.

2. How do you contact the sample? There are three basic ways: personal interview, phone survey, and mail. Each has its merits and its problems. Interviews can yield rich data, but they are expensive and difficult to carry out. Mail surveys are cheap and easy to conduct, but few people respond.

3. How do you ask the questions? Generally, the more specific the questions, the better. You want to avoid asking questions that are open to interpretation. If you cannot be sure what a person meant by a response, you will not be able to make sense of the results. For mail and phone surveys, **closed questions** (multiple choice) work best. For example, on a product survey, you might ask which types of soup participants eat by having them put a check by each item on a list of soups that they have eaten in the past. Closed questions make all of the answers consistent.

If you are unsure of what the answers will be, you can use **open questions** (essay). Instead of giving participants choices of how to answer, let them say whatever they want. For open questions, the interview format works best.

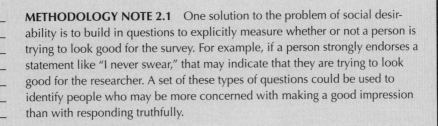

METHODOLOGY NOTE 2.1   One solution to the problem of social desirability is to build in questions to explicitly measure whether or not a person is trying to look good for the survey. For example, if a person strongly endorses a statement like "I never swear," that may indicate that they are trying to look good for the researcher. A set of these types of questions could be used to identify people who may be more concerned with making a good impression than with responding truthfully.

You also need to be sensitive to the ordering of the questions. Arrange them from general to specific to avoid fixing participants' responses early on. If you have several similar questions, mix them up so that you have several orderings over the whole set of surveys. Finally, use filter questions to cut down on the work of respondents (for example, "Do you own a car? If yes, then answer this set of car questions . . .").

It is especially important to avoid bias in the wording of the questions. Consider this item from a Democratic National Committee survey (1999): "Do you favor or oppose Republican plans to give parents tuition vouchers that would take tax dollars away from our public schools and use this money to subsidize tuition at private schools and academies?" It sounds like a "favor" response is bad, which may push respondents into saying "oppose." The authors of this survey are probably more interested in energizing the party faithful than in collecting real data (a significant amount of material in the brochure is devoted to appeals for money). That is fine as long as no attempt is made to generalize from the results to policy. If you really wanted to know how people felt about school vouchers, a less biased wording would be more appropriate.

4. How can you be sure that people are responding truthfully? Sometimes, people will feel pressure to lie to look good (a problem with **social desirability**; see Methodology Note 2.1). Other times, people may not know how to answer the question because they do not understand their own behavior. Any time you collect data using a survey, you have to worry about the accuracy of people's responses.

Ruback and Juieng (1997) investigated territorial behavior in the parking lot (this study was the target article for Chapter 1). They found that people take longer to back out of a space if someone is waiting. In their Study 3 they used a survey technique to determine if people are aware of their own territoriality. Previous research has suggested that they are not. For example, Ruback, Pape, and Doriot (1989) found that people did not think they would take longer at a pay phone when someone was waiting, even though people did take longer. For the parking lot study, Ruback and Juieng presented people with four questions about their behavior in the parking lot (similar questions are included in Chapter 1).

For themselves, people said intrusion would have more of an effect if the intrusion were more severe (if the waiting driver honked the horn). When thinking about another driver, the same pattern was present. Overall, people thought another driver would be more affected by intrusion than they would.

One interesting aspect of the questionnaire results is that the average response for a mild intrusion (no honking) was 2.35. That is on the "faster" end of the scale, suggesting that people think they will hurry up when another car is waiting. This aspect of their responding does not match with behavior, because people actually take longer. This may be due to a problem with social desirability. People know they take longer when someone is waiting, but they do not want to admit that to a researcher. It may also be a problem with people's self-knowledge. They may not be consciously aware of their behavior, and so they believe they are responding truthfully when they are not.

All of these issues were addressed by the author of our target article for this chapter. The topic was students' opinions about the grades they deserved in their classes.

- - - - - - -
Target Article: Grade Inflation

Are students' grade expectations in line with their performance in their classes? Or do students expect higher grades than their work would merit? The issue is grade inflation. This occurs when students' grades are higher than their performance warrants. Trout (1997) proposed that one reason for grade inflation is students' attitude that, as consumers of education, they should get something for their money (such as an A). Faculty may respond to this pressure because students complete evaluation forms. If students expect higher grades than their work merits, and they give lower evaluations because of that, faculty may give higher grades.

So, what are students' grade expectations? This question was addressed by our target article for this chapter (Landrum, 1999). The procedure was very simple. As part of the pilot testing of an evaluation instrument, Landrum asked students to rate the quality of their work in a class and to state their expected grade. Landrum was trying to see if students' expected grades matched their own assessment of the quality of their work.

Landrum's (1999) sample was 278 students from five courses. The faculty teaching these courses agreed to participate in the evaluation study. One question had students rate their performance on a scale labeled *Distinguished*, *Superior*, *Average*, *Below-Average*, and *Failure*. These were the university definitions of the five grade categories (A = *Distinguished*, etc.). A second question had students report their expected grade. There were also questions concerning the quality of the course, but those will not be discussed here.

Landrum (1999) found evidence for student expectation of grade inflation. Out of 159 students reporting that their own work was average, 115 (72%) expected a B or an A. This was in spite of the fact that the students were aware that C is the appropriate grade for average work. For 101 students reporting superior work (worthy of a B by definition), 41 (40%) expected an A.

A more direct comparison (to explicitly test for expectations of grade inflation) was provided by a paired *t* test. Expected grades and quality ratings were converted into GPAs for this test. The mean GPA for expected grade was 3.03. The mean GPA for quality of work was 2.43. This difference was significant [$t(275) = 14.16$, $p < .001$]. Landrum's (1999) results show that students do expect higher grades than their work would merit.

■ ■ ■ ■ ■ ■
Implementing the Design

Materials

You will not need any special materials for the projects below. For sampling purposes, you may want to obtain a campus directory that lists students and faculty. You may also need a random number table. You can also use the *Randomize Numbers* utility included with the software utilities for this book.

Suggested Projects

☆ 1. You can replicate Landrum's (1999) original survey by asking a sample of students on your campus about the quality of their work and their expected grades. Is there an expectation of grade inflation on your campus?

2. You can vary Landrum's (1999) procedure.

☆☆   a. It appears that Landrum (1999) invited all faculty to participate in his survey, and only five classes actually participated. This would not constitute a random sample of the population of students at his university. Maybe the professors who participated were also the ones who give more lenient grades (making them expect good evaluations). So, their students appear to expect higher grades than they ought to because they get higher grades than they ought to. Will students still expect grade inflation if a random sample is used?

☆☆☆   b. Instead of having students rate their own work, get a representative sample of their work and have an independent person rate it for quality. Students' grade expectations are too high according to their own estimates of the quality of their work. Are they even further off when an objective measure of quality is used?

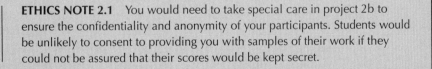

ETHICS NOTE 2.1 You would need to take special care in project 2b to ensure the confidentiality and anonymity of your participants. Students would be unlikely to consent to providing you with samples of their work if they could not be assured that their scores would be kept secret.

METHODOLOGY NOTE 2.2 To avoid biasing the raters in project 2b, you should remove any marks or grades before raters evaluate students' work.

☆☆ c. Are all students the same in their expectations for grade inflation, or are there differences? I can think of at least two student characteristics that may matter. The first is class year. Students new to college may not know what to expect. Perhaps seniors are more realistic in their expectations than freshmen. The second is major. Perhaps some departments are more lenient graders than others, creating the expectation of higher grades for poorer work. You could carry out Landrum's (1999) survey, but explicitly sample from different class years or different academic departments.

3. There are some other issues related to grade inflation that would be interesting.

☆☆☆ a. Where does the expectation of high grades for average work come from? You could sample students in different grades in school (first grade, third grade, etc.) and find out if there is a point where students come to expect more than they deserve (see Ethics Note 2.2).

☆☆☆ You might also try to find out *why* students expect higher grades than they should. You may need open-ended questions in a pilot study to collect a list of reasons. Then, use a closed question format to find out which reasons are the most important. You might also find some reasons by looking in the library. One hypothesis I have seen is that faculty perceive other universities as being more lenient. They feel that if they are overly strict, their students will be at a disadvantage when applying for graduate schools or jobs. So, they give higher grades to level the playing field. Is this also why students expect higher grades?

☆☆☆ b. Do faculty understand how grades are supposed to map onto work quality? Ask a sample of faculty to rate the quality of work for a hypothetical student and to estimate that student's grade. Is there an expectation of grade inflation?

ETHICS NOTE 2.2 Whenever you want to use a special population (like children), you will need to take special precautions to avoid any potential harm that may be unique to your population. Note that it will be especially difficult to get permission to conduct this type of research. The main problem is that children are not able to give informed consent. You will at least need consent from a parent. If the children are being recruited through a school, you will also need the school's permission. If you plan to use children as participants, know that your project will take longer to complete, and you should start the review process as early as possible.

☆☆☆   c. Trout (1997) proposes that fear of low evaluations causes faculty to give higher grades. Survey faculty to find out if this is true. Do they know about students' expectations? How do they respond to those expectations? Do they feel that their evaluations have been hurt based on their grading style?

■ ■ ■ ■ ■ ■
References

Consumer Reports. (1995, November). Mental health: Does therapy help? pp. 734–739.

Democratic National Committee. (1999). *1999 presidential agenda survey* [brochure]. Washington, DC: Author.

Landrum, R. E. (1999). Student expectations of grade inflation. *Journal of Research and Development in Education, 32,* 124–128. Used with permission of the author.

Ruback, R. B., & Juieng, D. (1997). Territorial defense in parking lots: Retaliation against waiting drivers. *Journal of Applied Social Psychology, 27,* 821–834.

Ruback, R. B., Pape, K., & Doriot, P. D. (1989). Waiting for a phone: Intrusion on callers leads to territorial defense. *Social Psychology Quarterly, 52,* 232–241.

Seligman, M. E. P. (1995). The effectiveness of psychotherapy: The *Consumer Reports* study. *American Psychologist, 50,* 965–974.

Trout, P. A. (1997). Disengaged students and the decline of academic standards. *Academic Questions, 10,* 46–56.

Correlation Research

Stressed? Take two dogs and call me in the morning

Is owning a pet related to one's stress or health? Research has shown that petting a companion dog can lower blood pressure (Vormbrock & Grossberg, 1988). Pet ownership has also been related to better survival after discharge from a coronary care unit (Friedmann, Katcher, Lynch, & Thomas, 1980). Our target article for this chapter investigated the relationship between pet ownership and visits to the doctor for senior citizens (Siegel, 1990). Owning a pet was related to making fewer doctor visits over a period of one year.

▪▪▪▪▪▪ Introduction: Finding Relationships

One goal of research in any scientific discipline is to find out what relationships exist between variables in the world. In Chapter 1, we looked at how observation of naturally occurring behavior could be used to uncover relationships. In Chapter 2, we looked at how survey data could be used to uncover relationships.

Correlation research is a special case of observation and survey research. Three things characterize correlation research. The first characteristic is that all of the variables are measured variables. The investigator does not manipulate anything that is being studied. The second characteristic is that the variables being measured must be capable of being expressed numerically, and the more values the variables can take on, the better. (Ideally, the variables will be **continuous**. A continuous variable has an infinite number of possible values, such as height.) The third characteristic is the computation of a correlation coefficient once the data are collected. A correlation coefficient can tell us the strength and direction of a relationship.

Let's consider an example of a correlational study. Daneman and Carpenter (1980) were interested in the relationship between one's ability to understand written text passages and a variable called "reading span." To measure reading span, a person is given a list of sentences to read out loud and then has to memorize the last word in each sentence. After a set of sentences, the person has to report the last words. For example, a set of two sentences would be:

1. According to the results of the survey, Robert Redford is the most-liked Hollywood star.
2. The weather was unpredictable that summer, so no one made plans too far in advance.

A person being tested would read the sentences and then recall "star" and "advance." The sentences can be presented in sets of 2, 3, 4, 5, or 6; a person's reading span is the largest number of sentences for which he or she can recall the final words.

The goal of developing the reading span test is to find a quick method of assessing a person's working memory capacity. Then, the test could be used to sort participants in reading experiments into high- and low-capacity groups or to control for differences in capacity. To assess reading comprehension, Daneman and Carpenter (1980) had participants read short stories and answer questions about them. To see if the span test was related to this measure of comprehension ability, Daneman and Carpenter computed the correlation between reading span and people's ability to answer the questions correctly. This correlation was $r = .72$. What does that mean?

First, a correlation can range between -1 and $+1$. A positive correlation means that a positive relationship exists. As the score on one measured variable increases, so does the score on the other. In the case of reading span and comprehension, there is a positive relationship, so as reading span gets higher, so does comprehension. A negative correlation means that a negative relationship exists between two variables. As a score on one increases, the score on the other decreases.

A large correlation has an absolute value close to 1. So, .72 is relatively large (note that $-.72$ would be just as large, the sign is irrelevant when considering the size of a correlation). The larger the correlation, the stronger the relationship.

What we can say, then, is that a strong positive relationship exists between reading span and text comprehension. Does this mean that a big reading span causes improved comprehension? No. You need to commit this fact to memory and keep it fresh in your mind: Correlation does not imply causation. All we know after we compute a correlation is that a relationship exists. Causally, there are three possible situations. In terms of span and comprehension:

1. High spans cause good comprehension (high-span people have so much mental room that they can simultaneously read and hold more ideas from a text, improving comprehension).
2. People who comprehend well have high spans (maybe because they are not working so hard to understand the sentences, they have room left over to hold the words).

3. Some third factor causes people to have high spans and comprehend well (for example, a good diet helps all cognitive capacities to improve).

With just a correlation, each possibility is equally likely to be true, and we have no way of telling which is correct. We cannot use a correlation to establish causality.

So, correlation research can be used to determine the strength and direction of relationships between variables. But you cannot use correlation research to uncover information about the causes of behavior. You may be asking yourself, "Why would anyone do correlation research if a causal statement cannot be made at the end of the study?" There are three good reasons.

1. *Ethics.* If I wanted to investigate the relationship between self-esteem and body image, I could randomly assign one group to be low in self-esteem, but that would require me to lower their self-esteem. This would violate ethical principles. Similarly, it would not be possible to manipulate childhood sexual abuse to investigate its effect on adult psychological well-being. To investigate these questions, we would have to do correlational research.
2. *Generalizability.* A good experiment requires careful control by the experimenter. Achieving this control can reduce the naturalness of the task. If an experimenter wants the conditions of the research to closely match those in the real world, a correlation design may be chosen.
3. *Feasibility.* Experiments can be difficult and expensive to conduct. The corresponding correlation research might be simpler because participant populations are readily available. In those cases, researchers do correlation research to fully explore the relationship between two variables. Once the relationship is understood, it is then possible to do an experiment to determine causality.

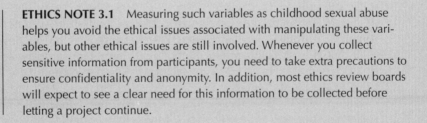

ETHICS NOTE 3.1 Measuring such variables as childhood sexual abuse helps you avoid the ethical issues associated with manipulating these variables, but other ethical issues are still involved. Whenever you collect sensitive information from participants, you need to take extra precautions to ensure confidentiality and anonymity. In addition, most ethics review boards will expect to see a clear need for this information to be collected before letting a project continue.

Our target article for this chapter used a correlation approach for a combination of the second and third reasons. Siegel (1990) was interested in the relationship between owning pets and physical well-being. She used a naturally occurring sample of pet owners and non-pet owners to look at the relationship because this generalizes better to the natural situation and because this was more efficient than assigning people to pet ownership conditions.

■ ■ ■ ■ ■ ■

Target Article: The Relationship Between Pet Ownership and Health

A number of studies have found a relationship between pet ownership and health. Friedmann et al. (1980) found that pet owners had a higher survival rate after discharge from a coronary care unit compared to non–pet owners. Baun, Bergstrom, Langston, and Thoma (1983) found that petting a companion dog produced the greatest reduction in blood pressure over time (compared to petting a strange dog or reading a magazine). Vormbrock and Grossberg (1988) also found that touching a dog could lower blood pressure to resting levels. They suggest that petting a dog could have therapeutic benefits for patients who feel isolated.

There is also evidence that pet ownership can reduce stress. Fritz, Farver, Hart, and Kass (1996) found that pet ownership may reduce stress in people taking care of Alzheimer patients (although some of their findings were mixed). Allen, Blascovich, Tomaka, and Kelsey (1991) had women perform a stressful task (counting backwards) and measured arousal. The women performed the task in a laboratory setting, at home alone, at home with a pet dog, or at home with a close female friend. The results were that doing the task in the presence of a pet dog produced the lowest levels of stress. Allen et al. interpreted their results as showing that the benefit of a pet may be due to the nonevaluative nature of the relationship.

Cohen and Williamson (1991) reviewed the literature on the relationship between stress and disease and found that higher stress leads to higher illness behavior (symptoms and doctor visits). Given this linkage, it seems reasonable to suspect that something that reduces stress (like having a companion animal) will also reduce illness behavior. That was the approach taken by our target article (Siegel, 1990). The question was: Is there a relationship between owning a pet and visits to the doctor?

Siegel (1990) used a survey methodology to collect information about her sample. The details of survey research were covered in Chapter 2. We will consider only the highlights of her methodology here. Her sample was composed of 1,034 enrollees in an HMO in California. The participants were interviewed prior to the study to collect demographic information. This included health questions, gender, age, racial-ethnic group, income, education, marital status, social network, and pet ownership. Of the original sample, 938 completed the entire study.

_____ **METHODOLOGY NOTE 3.1**   Siegel's (1990) research incorporates some
_____ features that cannot be replicated within a single semester as a research
_____ methods project. The list of suggested projects for this chapter contains some
_____ ideas that are based on Siegel's work but that can be completed in less time.

Participants were interviewed every two months for a year. The main question concerned the number of trips to the doctor in each two-month period. At intervals during the year, depression and stressful life events were assessed as well. Pet owners were also asked questions about their relationship with their pet.

Siegel (1990) conducted a multiple regression analysis on her data. In multiple regression the goal is to explain the variance in people's scores (differences in scores). As you probably already know, every person is different from every other person. If we had a complete psychological theory, we could explain all of those differences. In the absence of a complete theory, we explain as many differences as we can. The main type of difference for Siegel to explain was number of doctor visits. Why do some people go more often than others? She proposed that pet ownership will explain some of the differences in number of doctor visits.

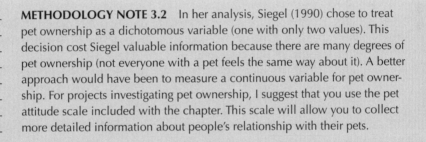

METHODOLOGY NOTE 3.2   In her analysis, Siegel (1990) chose to treat pet ownership as a dichotomous variable (one with only two values). This decision cost Siegel valuable information because there are many degrees of pet ownership (not everyone with a pet feels the same way about it). A better approach would have been to measure a continuous variable for pet ownership. For projects investigating pet ownership, I suggest that you use the pet attitude scale included with the chapter. This scale will allow you to collect more detailed information about people's relationship with their pets.

The first step for Siegel (1990) was to enter into her regression all of the demographic variables. By taking out the variability due to things like gender, age, and marital status, she essentially equated all of the people on those factors. Then, she looked at the relationship with pet ownership. There was a significant negative relationship between pet ownership and number of doctor visits. In other words, people with pets went to the doctor fewer times. This was also true of the subset of doctor's visits initiated by the patients themselves.

Note that we cannot make any causal conclusions from this. In other words, we cannot say that having a pet will cause a person to visit the doctor less often. All we can say for sure is that a relationship exists.

Siegel (1990) notes that the life events that were particularly common were loss events (death of a close family member or friend). This might create a need for companionship that a pet could fill. In terms of causality, this provides one alternative explanation. People with pets might go to the doctor less often because they are actually healthier, or they might go less often because they are less lonely (assuming that a doctor visit can fill a need for personal interaction). This is the sort of issue that cannot be resolved using correlational research.

■ ■ ■ ■ ■ ■

Implementing the Design

Materials

Some materials to help you with projects in this area are included in the supplements at the end of the chapter. These materials include:

1. *A pet attitude scale (adapted from Templer, Salter, Dickey, Baldwin, & Veleber, 1981).* Only the scale and scoring instructions are included here. Their original article contains information on how the scale was developed and which aspects of pet ownership it can assess.
2. *Some of the scales used by Siegel (1990).* The items on the life events scale and her assessment of pet attitude are included.

Some other scales that might also be useful are:

1. *A stress index.*
2. *The CES-D scale (Radloff, 1977).* This was used by Siegel (1990) to assess depression. Depression was not an important factor in her study, but it might be a valuable measure in a study designed to understand the specific benefits of pet ownership.
3. *The Lubben Social Network Scale (Lubben, 1988).* Siegel (1990) used this scale to measure how connected people are to a social network. You might also need this scale to assess social contact.

If you want to use any scales that are not included in the supplements, be sure to check your library for availability early in your project. You may need to order a copy through interlibrary loan, which could take a few weeks.

METHODOLOGY NOTE 3.3   Some of the projects suggested in this chapter may more accurately be described as quasi experiments than correlation designs. In a true experiment, all of the variables are manipulated (see Chapter 4 for more on this). In a quasi experiment, variables are not manipulated, but specific values are chosen (for example, pet owner or not). If a design included a manipulated variable and a nonmanipulated variable, that design would also be a quasi experiment. The main difference between a quasi experiment and a correlation design is the restriction to only a few values of one of the variables. It is almost as if some variable is being manipulated, because we have chosen certain values to observe, but we are still only *measuring* the variables. This limits causal conclusions in the same way that using a correlational design will limit causal conclusions. For that reason, I have included some quasi-experimental designs in the project list. In most cases, the appropriate analysis will still be a correlation, and everything that has been said above about correlation designs will apply.

Suggested Projects

1. You will be unable to replicate the original research in the time allotted for Research Methods. However, you can replicate aspects of it. Some suggestions:

   ☆ a. A simple project would be to use some of the same measures as Siegel (1990) in a student population. Instead of asking questions over a year-long interval, you can ask people to think back as far as you would like. So, you could ask people, "Within the last six months, how many times have you been sick?" Then, correlate that with Siegel's measures of pet relationship.

   ☆ b. You could use a stress scale as the dependent variable (instead of illnesses) and look at the correlation between currently perceived stress and pet relationship.

   ☆☆ c. You could create your own stress scale based on a modification of Siegel's life events scale. You could include items like "How stressful have midterm exams been for you?" Make a seven-point scale for each item. Then, instead of simply counting life events, you can assess their impact on a person. Does the impact correlate with pet relationship?

   ☆ d. In the projects above, use the pet attitude scale in Supplement 1 instead of Siegel's pet relationship items.

   ☆☆ e. Incorporate other populations. The projects above suggest using students because they are a population to which you have ready access. Siegel (1990) used senior citizens. If you have access to a similar population, you could conduct a modified version of Siegel's research. Fritz et al. (1996) found differences based on sex (men and women were affected differently by pets) and age (younger people were affected differently than older people). Siegel found differences based on type of pet. Are there "cat people" and "dog people"? Do the differences in type of pet reflect the fit between the type of person and the pet (such as, dog people do better with dogs)?

2. You might also try a project investigating therapeutic aspects of pet ownership (these will be harder to conduct).

   ☆☆☆ a. Siegel (1993) suggests a functional approach to studying the relationship between pet ownership and life events. For example, are pets always beneficial, or only in times of severe stress? Are there times when pet ownership would actually be a burden? There are some populations that actually do worse when pets are present. Beck and Katcher (1984) cite a study showing that rural women experience a decrease in health when they have pets. They also note that the relationship between criminal activity and animal cruelty might mitigate the value of pet therapy in prisons or with juvenile delinquents. What are the relationships between pets and stress/health in populations like these?

   ☆☆☆ b. Siegel (1993) notes that the benefits of pet-facilitated therapy are usually based on anecdotal evidence. In pet-facilitated therapy, a pet is actually introduced into a home instead of measuring a naturally occurring

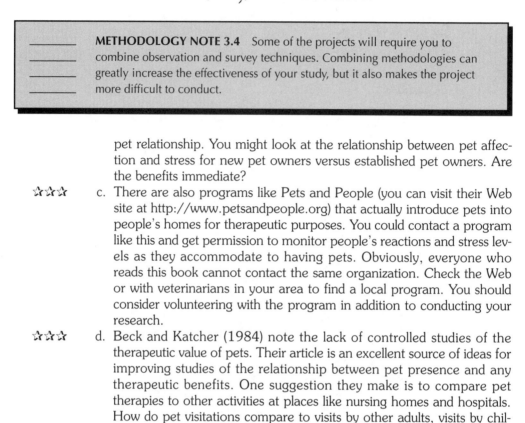

METHODOLOGY NOTE 3.4   Some of the projects will require you to combine observation and survey techniques. Combining methodologies can greatly increase the effectiveness of your study, but it also makes the project more difficult to conduct.

pet relationship. You might look at the relationship between pet affection and stress for new pet owners versus established pet owners. Are the benefits immediate?

☆☆☆   c. There are also programs like Pets and People (you can visit their Web site at http://www.petsandpeople.org) that actually introduce pets into people's homes for therapeutic purposes. You could contact a program like this and get permission to monitor people's reactions and stress levels as they accommodate to having pets. Obviously, everyone who reads this book cannot contact the same organization. Check the Web or with veterinarians in your area to find a local program. You should consider volunteering with the program in addition to conducting your research.

☆☆☆   d. Beck and Katcher (1984) note the lack of controlled studies of the therapeutic value of pets. Their article is an excellent source of ideas for improving studies of the relationship between pet presence and any therapeutic benefits. One suggestion they make is to compare pet therapies to other activities at places like nursing homes and hospitals. How do pet visitations compare to visits by other adults, visits by children, the introduction of video games, or ice cream socials? An important consideration of pet therapy that has not been discussed so far is the potential negative impact of bites and disease that comes along with introducing pets. If pet therapy does not produce more of an effect than other methods, should it still be used?

☆☆   e. Siegel (1993) also suggests looking at people who do not like pets. Is there any benefit to pet-facilitated therapy among non–pet lovers? You could focus your study on people who report a low level of pet attachment (such as the roommate of a person with a pet). How is pet presence related to that person's stress level?

ETHICS NOTE 3.2   Whenever you wish to work with some outside agency to conduct your research, you need to get permission using a process similar to getting informed consent from participants. Some issues to consider: What are the benefits of the research? What risks are involved? How have you tried to minimize the risks? How will participants be informed about the research? Treat the people who will help you as research partners, and explain the entire project to them at the beginning. This will make it easier to get permission and will help you to conduct research in an ethical manner.

    f. You might look at which components of the pet relationship are most related to reduced stress. Some suggestions (primarily from Siegel, 1993):

☆☆   (1) *Attachment and bonding.* People may substitute strong bonds with pets for poor bonding with humans. This would suggest investigating people's social networks to look at the correlations among pet attachment, amount of social involvement, and stress.

☆☆   (2) *Nonjudgmental love.* Pets do not evaluate their owners; they provide unconditional affection. Perhaps it is the unconditional nature of the love that reduces stress (Allen et al., 1991, found some support for this). Is the relationship between pet ownership and reduced stress stronger for dogs than cats because dogs are perceived as being less judgmental?

☆☆   (3) *Touching.* People tend to touch more in pet relationships than in human relationships, and touching can be therapeutic. Maybe the appropriate correlation would be between amount of pet touching and stress.

☆☆☆ 3. *Participant observation.* Another suggestion would be to do a participant observation of pet owners to find out about their relationship with their pets. Look for a correlation between your observed pet attachment and self-reported stress. You could find out if people's reported pet attachment matches their actual behavior with their pet. Or, by observing, you may get a better idea of which components of the pet relationship might contribute to stress reduction.

■ ■ ■ ■ ■ ■
References

Allen, K. M., Blascovich, J., Tomaka, J., & Kelsey, R. M. (1991). Presence of human friends and pet dogs as moderators of autonomic responses to stress in women. *Journal of Personality and Social Psychology, 61,* 582–589.

Baun, M. M., Bergstrom, N., Langston, N. F., & Thoma, L. (1984). Physiological effects of human/companion animal bonding. *Nursing Research, 33,* 126–129.

Beck, A. M., & Katcher, A. H. (1984). A new look at pet-facilitated therapy. *Journal of the American Veterinary Medical Association, 184,* 414–421.

Cohen, S., & Williamson, G. M. (1991). Stress and infectious disease in humans. *Psychological Bulletin, 109,* 5–24.

Daneman, M., & Carpenter, P. A. (1980). Individual differences in working memory and reading. *Journal of Verbal Learning and Verbal Behavior, 19,* 450–466.

Friedmann, E., Katcher, A. H., Lynch, J. J., & Thomas, S. A. (1980). Animal companions and one-year survival of patients after discharge from a coronary care unit. *Public Health Reports, 95,* 307–312.

Fritz, C. L., Farver, T. B., Hart, L. A., & Kass, P. H. (1996). Companion animals and the psychological health of Alzheimer patients' caregivers. *Psychological Reports, 78,* 467–481.

Lubben, J. E. (1988). Assessing social networks among elderly populations. *Journal of Family and Community Health, 11,* 42–52.

Radloff, L. S. (1977). The CES-D scale: A self-report depression scale for research in the general population. *Applied Psychological Measurement, 1,* 385–401.

Siegel, J. M. (1990). Stressful life events and use of physician services among the elderly: The moderating role of pet ownership. *Journal of Personality and Social Psychology, 58,* 1081–1086. Used with permission of the author.

Siegel, J. M. (1993). Companion animals: In sickness and in health. *Journal of Social Issues, 49,* 157–167.

Templer, D. I., Salter, C. A., Dickey, S., Baldwin, R., & Veleber, D. M. (1981). The construction of a pet attitude scale. *The Psychological Record, 31,* 343–348.

Vormbrock, J. K., & Grossberg, J. M. (1988). Cardiovascular effects of human–pet dog interactions. *Journal of Behavioral Medicine, 11,* 509–517.

Pet Attitude Scale

For each item below, choose the number that best matches your feelings about the item.

Strongly disagree			Neither agree nor disagree			Strongly agree
1	2	3	4	5	6	7

1. _____   1. I really like seeing pets enjoy their food.

2. _____   2. My pet means more to me than any of my friends.

3. _____   3. I would like a pet in my home.

4. _____   4. Having pets is a waste of money.

5. _____   5. House pets add happiness to my life (or would if I had one).

6. _____   6. I feel that pets should always be kept outside.

7. _____   7. I spend time every day playing with my pet (or would if I had one).

8. _____   8. I have occasionally communicated with a pet and understood what it was trying to express.

9. _____   9. The world would be a better place if people would stop spending so much time caring for their pets and started caring more for other human beings instead.

10. _____   10. I like to feed animals out of my hand.

11. _____   11. I love pets.

12. _____   12. Animals belong in the wild or in zoos, but not in the home.

13. _____   13. If you keep pets in your house, you can expect a lot of damage to furniture.

14. _____   14. I like house pets.

15. _____   15. Pets are fun but it's not worth the trouble of owning one.

16. _____   16. I frequently talk to my pet.

17. _____   17. I hate animals.

18. _____   18. You should treat your house pets with as much respect as you would a human member of your family.

For scoring, add up the total for items 1, 2, 3, 5, 7, 8, 10, 11, 14, 16, and 18. Then, reverse score items 4, 6, 9, 12, 13, 15, and 17 (if the person wrote 7, change it to 1, for 6 make it 2, etc.). Then, add up the reversed scores. Add the two totals together; that is the person's pet attitude score. Scores can range from 18 to 126. The higher the score, the more positive the person's feelings are toward pets.

Additional Scales

Life Events Scale

In the last 6 months, I have experienced (mark all that apply):

_____ A separation or divorce

_____ The death of a close family member

_____ A major illness of my spouse

_____ A retirement

_____ The death of a close friend

_____ A move

_____ Being the victim of a crime

_____ Having a relative be the victim of a crime

_____ Being denied a driver's license

_____ Money problems

Pet Relationship

Pet responsibility

For each, use this scale: Respondent Alone, Respondent and Some Other Person, or Some Other Person Alone

1. Whose decision was it to get the pet? _____

2. Who is most responsible for the care and feeding, including trips to the veterinarian?

_____

Time spent with pet

For item 1, use this scale: Almost Never or a Little, Some, Most or All of the Time

1. How much time are you and your pet in the same room when you are at home? _____

_____

2. How many hours per day are you outdoors with your pet? _____

3. How many hours per day do you spend petting your pet? _____

4. How many hours per day do you spend talking to your pet? _____

For item 5, use this scale: Much Less or a Little Less, About the Same, a Little More or Much More

5. How much time do you spend with your pet compared to other people you know

   with pets? _____

Affective attachment

1. Would you say your pet is: extremely important to you, very important to you, fairly important to you, not too important to you, or not at all important to you? _____

_____

Benefits and costs

1. What are the benefits of having a pet? _____

_____

_____

2. What are the costs of having a pet? _____

_____

_____

Source: Adapted from "Stressful life events and use of physician services among the elderly: The moderating role of pet ownership," by J. M. Siegel, 1990, *Journal of Personality and Social Psychology, 58,* 1081–1086. Copyright © 1990 by the American Psychological Association. Adapted with permission.

Part Two

Experimental Designs

The research techniques in Part Two all involve manipulating some aspect of the situation to determine its effect on behavior. The experimental designs start with the simplest possible situation (two groups) and move to more complex designs (factorial designs). Field experiments are basically the same experimental techniques applied in a real-world setting.

CHAPTER 4

Two-Group Experiments

Strooped again!

The Stroop effect was named for J. Ridley Stroop, who originally described it in 1935. The basic experiment involves two tasks. In one task, people name the colors of color words written in mismatching ink colors (e.g., the word *red* in blue ink). In the other task, people name the colors of colored boxes. Naming the colors of mismatching color words is harder. Recently, the Stroop effect has been used as an index of other psychological phenomena. For example, Cooper and Todd (1997) found different amounts of Stroop interference for people with three types of eating disorders.

■■■■■■
Introduction: What Is an Experiment?

Until now, the methods we have used have allowed us only to describe relationships that exist between two variables. For example, we could observe that the time it takes people to back out of a parking space is related to whether or not someone is waiting for the space. We have not been able to say that one variable caused a change in another variable. To do that, we need to do an experiment, and that is the topic of this chapter.

There are three components of an experiment:

1. Manipulate something.
2. Measure something (this component is present for all designs).
3. Random assignment.

Let's consider each in turn. Unlike the designs in Part One, we will actually choose some variable to manipulate and control its presentation. As an example, instead of watching for a car to wait for a space and then beginning our observation, we would manipulate whether or not a car was present. Choosing what to manipulate can be difficult. Careful work with observation, survey, or correlation designs can reduce the burden by suggesting which variables are related.

You are already familiar with measurement from the designs in Part One. Let's introduce some new terminology. The variable that we manipulate is called the **independent variable**. It is independent because we can choose to manipulate anything. The variable we measure will be the **dependent variable**. It is dependent because its value depends on the value of the independent variable that we have presented. As an example, consider the parking lot. Whether or not a car is waiting would be the independent variable. Time to back out would be the dependent variable. Time depends on the independent variable, because it should take longer if another car is present.

Random assignment is probably the most important component of an experiment. It ensures that each participant in the experiment has an equal chance of being in either group. For a two-group experiment, one way to do random assignment would be to flip a coin as each person arrives to participate. Heads would be group 1, tails would be group 2.

Why is random assignment so important? We need to be certain that the groups in an experiment are equal before we begin. We could try to match them to make sure they are equal, but people differ from one another in an infinite number of ways. No matter how carefully we match, there would always be the possibility that some systematic difference exists. By using random assignment, we reduce any systematic biases that may exist. (Random assignment will not guarantee equal groups; it just guarantees that the selection process itself is unbiased.)

The simplest type of experiment is the two-group experiment. Usually, one group is called a **treatment group** because it receives some treatment. The other group is called the **control group** because it receives no treatment. If the experiment is well conducted, the only difference between the treatment and control groups is that one got a treatment and one did not. If you compare scores on the dependent variable for the two groups and the scores are different, then you can conclude that the treatment caused the difference.

How do you know what to manipulate to create treatment and control groups? The problem is in coming up with a good **operational definition**. This is a definition of the treatment in terms of the operations required to pro-

---

METHODOLOGY NOTE 4.1   When choosing a control group, a special concern is something called a **placebo effect**. People might be affected by their knowledge of how the independent variable is supposed to affect them and not by the independent variable itself. For example, people know how they are supposed to behave after consuming alcohol, so they may behave that way even if the alcohol itself is not producing the behavior. To prevent this, we should make both groups think they are receiving the same treatment. After the experiment, we will know that any differences are due to the treatment and not placebo effects.

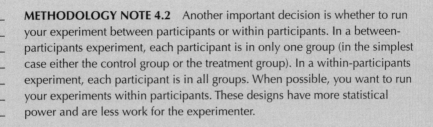

METHODOLOGY NOTE 4.2   Another important decision is whether to run your experiment between participants or within participants. In a between-participants experiment, each participant is in only one group (in the simplest case either the control group or the treatment group). In a within-participants experiment, each participant is in all groups. When possible, you want to run your experiments within participants. These designs have more statistical power and are less work for the experimenter.

duce or measure it. An operational definition creates a very concrete description of the conditions of an experiment.

Let's examine the properties of an experiment by looking at research investigating the Stroop effect.

■ ■ ■ ■ ■ ■
Target Article: The Stroop Effect

The original experiment was performed by J. Ridley Stroop in 1935. Since then, this has become one of the most famous effects in all of psychology (MacLeod, 1991, 1992). The effect is very simple to describe. When people are asked to name the colors of words, their naming performance is slowed compared to naming the colors of blocks of color (such as a blue rectangle). The more the words interfere with color naming, the harder the task is. The hardest condition of all is when the words are color names (e.g., *red*) in different colors from the ones being named (e.g., the word *red* in blue ink).

This effect is often attributed to a response competition problem. When the word and the color do not match, there are two possible color responses available ("red" and "blue" in the example above). Because reading is so well practiced, the written response ("red") gets through faster than the color of the ink (blue). In other words, the wrong response is more readily available. The competition between these two responses slows people down and causes them to make a lot of mistakes. In the control condition, there is no competition, so responding is relatively fast and error free. This is the sort of explanation Stroop (1935) proposed, but other explanations are also possible. For a complete discussion, see MacLeod (1991).

Experiment 1

In his Experiment 1, Stroop (1935) presented the color words *red*, *blue*, *green*, *brown*, and *purple*. In the mismatch condition, each color word appeared equally often in the other four ink colors, but never in the matching color. In the control condition, each word was written in black ink. In this

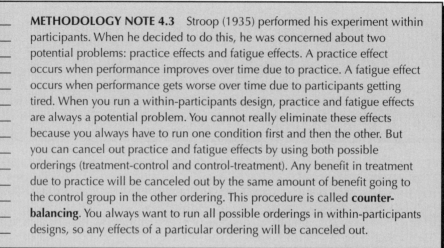

METHODOLOGY NOTE 4.3   Stroop (1935) performed his experiment within participants. When he decided to do this, he was concerned about two potential problems: practice effects and fatigue effects. A practice effect occurs when performance improves over time due to practice. A fatigue effect occurs when performance gets worse over time due to participants getting tired. When you run a within-participants design, practice and fatigue effects are always a potential problem. You cannot really eliminate these effects because you always have to run one condition first and then the other. But you can cancel out practice and fatigue effects by using both possible orderings (treatment-control and control-treatment). Any benefit in treatment due to practice will be canceled out by the same amount of benefit going to the control group in the other ordering. This procedure is called **counter-balancing**. You always want to run all possible orderings in within-participants designs, so any effects of a particular ordering will be canceled out.

experiment, participants were instructed to read the words, not name the colors of the ink (a difference from what is described above). Participants read 200 words in the mismatch condition and 200 in the control condition.

The results were that there was no difference in reading the words. Overall, participants took 2.3 seconds longer in the mismatch condition, but the difference was not significant.

Experiment 2

The same word stimuli were used as in the first experiment, but the control condition was a sheet of colored rectangles in the same five colors. The task now was to name the color of the ink, not read the word. There were 200 stimuli in each condition.

The results were that there was a big difference in naming time. Participants took 47 seconds longer in the mismatching condition.

What we have so far is that mismatching colors do not disrupt reading, but they really interfere with color naming. This is enough to see why the Stroop effect is often seen as showing that reading is automatic. Reading is such an overlearned response that people can do it well even when the ink colors do

METHODOLOGY NOTE 4.4   Note how the control group had to change for Stroop's (1935) Experiment 2 to provide the appropriate baseline for color naming. If participants had read the words in black ink as in Experiment 1, the experiment would have been comparing apples and oranges (reading vs. color naming). Instead, a new control group was devised that involved color naming but had no interference.

not match the words. But when they are doing a unique task such as naming colors, reading gets in the way, because the meaning of the word itself gets through faster than the ink color.

You may be thinking to yourself, so reading is automatic, so what? When we get to the projects, you will see that this effect can be used in clinical assessment. In outline, imagine that you want to assess a person's generalized anxiety. You could ask that person to name the colors of threat words (e.g., *stress*) and neutral words (e.g., *tree*). If there is more Stroop interference for the threat words, you know those words must be more "on" the person's mind. It is so hard to avoid reading the meaning of the words that it slows down their color naming.

■ ■ ■ ■ ■ ■
Implementing the Design

Materials

You may implement Stroop experiments in one of two ways. The first way is to create stimulus cards (with a color printer). You will need three kinds of stimuli to replicate Stroop's experiments: color words in black, color words in mismatching colors, and colored rectangles. You should create at least two cards for each to avoid confounds due to word order. You will also need a stopwatch for this option. Simply present participants with the appropriate card, time them as they do the task, and record the time. For some of the projects below, you will need to create additional stimulus cards.

You may also use the software provided with this chapter to present the experiments in the projects section. There are several steps involved. First, you have to either choose from the sample stimuli or create your own. Then, you have to set up your experiment using the software. Once the data are collected, you will have to use the analysis software to view the results.

■ The *Stroop Task* Software

To implement your own experiments you will need the *Stroop Task* software. This software allows you to implement the original Stroop experiments. You may also customize the software to present your own experiments. Follow the installation instructions in Appendix E to install the software from the CD.

❑ *Setting Up the Stimuli*
Using the sample stimuli   The first component of any Stroop experiment is the stimuli. You may use the stimulus sets provided, or you may create your own. The sets that are included with the software are described in Table 4.1.

Creating your own stimuli   The stimuli for the Stroop experiment are all picture files. For presenting words, this may seem like overkill, but some of the

Table 4.1 List of Stimuli Provided with the *Stroop Task* Software*

Folder	Stimuli
Stroop Stimuli E1	
Cond1	Color words in black
Cond2	Mismatching color words (*blue* in red, etc.)
Prac	"R," "G," "Y," "B" in black
Sample Stimuli	
Cond1	Mismatching color words (*blue* in red, etc.)
Cond2	Colored rectangles
Cond3	Matching color words (*blue* in blue, etc.)
Cond4	Mismatching pseudowords (*bloo* in red, etc.)
Cond5	Number words in colors
Prac	"R," "G," "Y," "B" in black
Project Stimuli	
Cond1	Spider words in colors
Cond2	Neutral spider words
Prac	"R," "G," "Y," "B" in black

*For Macintosh users, opening a stimulus folder and viewing by icon will give you a preview of the stimuli without opening the files.

projects require pictures as stimuli. The way the program is designed, anything that can be made into a picture can be presented. This will make your task a little harder as you create your own stimuli, but it will also give you more flexibility in what you can present.

To create your own stimuli, you need to follow these rules:

1. All stimuli need to be saved as PICT files for Macintosh users, or .BMP files for Windows users. You should have only one stimulus per file. You may use any paint or drawing program to make stimuli. The file should contain only the stimulus. Any white areas around the stimulus should be trimmed.

A good Macintosh utility for modifying stimuli is a program called *GraphicConverter*™. Using this program, choose "Trim" from the "Edit" menu to remove extra white areas. Then, save as PICT. For Windows users, create the stimuli using the *Paint* program that comes with Windows. In that program, select the stimulus and choose "Copy To" from the "Edit" menu. This will allow you to save only the selected area.

2. The stimuli for a given experiment should all be in the same folder. The practice stimuli should also be in this folder.

3. All stimuli should be named "Cond#Stim#". Cond# refers to the condition number. If you have colored words and colored boxes, the condition numbers might be 1 for words and 2 for boxes. Stim# is the stimulus number in the condition. Number them sequentially, keeping in mind that the stimuli will be interpreted by the program as follows:

First fourth RED
Second fourth GREEN
Third fourth YELLOW
Fourth fourth BLUE

If you are having trouble getting the program to score your stimuli correctly, this is probably the problem. Check to make sure that:

1. You have the same number of stimuli in all conditions. (Pad with duplicates if necessary.)
2. The stimuli are numbered according to this rule.

Once you have your stimuli prepared, you are ready to run the program. There are two modes in which you can run the program.

❏ *Running an Experiment That Is Already Set Up*

To run Stroop's (1935) Experiment 1 or 2, open the "Experiments" folder and double-click the experiment you want. If you run a standard experiment, the program will automatically load the correct parameters. All you need to do is enter a participant number and press "Enter." If you have already programmed your own experiment, double-clicking its parameter file will produce the same effect.

❏ *Setting Up an Experiment*

To program your own experiment, double-click the *Stroop Task* program. When the experiment is running, click the "Set Up" button. This will take you to the program's parameter screen.

There are three types of parameters that you will need to set before running an experiment. Stimulus parameters tell the program how many stimuli to present and where they are located. Practice parameters tell the program how to implement practice trials. Presentation parameters tell the program how to implement the experiment. Each will be discussed in turn.

Setting the stimulus parameters   Click the "Change" button by "Stimulus Parameters." You will get the screen in Figure 4.1.

Enter the number of conditions in your experiment and the number of stimuli per condition (this is the number of unique stimuli, not the number of trials you plan to present). Also enter the number of practice stimuli. Usually, you will use the "R," "G," "Y," and "B" from the "Sample Stimuli" folder as practice stimuli. If you use any other stimuli for practice, you will have to present custom instructions.

You can choose to have all of the stimuli presented as the same size (approximately 2″ × 3″), or as their original size (up to a maximum of 2″ × 3″). To stretch all of the stimuli to fit into the same size window, click "Stretch stimuli . . ." (This option is not available to Macintosh users.)

Finally, click "Find Stimuli" and open any stimulus file in the correct folder. The path to the stimuli will appear in the box. Any time you launch from these

Figure 4.1 *Stroop Task* stimulus parameters screen.

Change Stroop stimulus parameters

[2]   stimulus conditions with [12]   stimuli per condition
[4]   practice stimuli

☐ Stretch stimuli to fit 2" high X 3" wide window

Rules for making stimuli:
1. Save the stimuli as '.BMP' files.
2. Name the files 'Cond#Stim#' The first number is the number of the condition, the second number is the number of the stimulus within the condition.
3. Save the practice stimuli as 'PracStim#' They should be in the same folder as the main stimuli.

Click the 'Find Stimuli' button to open any stimulus file. The path will be displayed below. That path will be used to find all stimuli when the program runs.   [Find Stimuli]

The current data path is C:\WINDOWS\Desktop\Stroop\Stimuli\Stroop Stimuli E1\

[Cancel]   [Done]

settings, the program will always follow this path to find the stimuli. If you move folders around after setting the path, you will need to do this step again. So, do not perform this step until you have all of the stimulus folders where you want to leave them. As long as the folders are located in the same place on all machines, you can set up parameters on one machine and use the same paths on other machines. The best approach is to leave all stimulus folders in the "Stroop Task" folder.

Click "Done" to return to the parameters screen.

Setting the practice parameters   Click the "Change" button by "Practice Parameters." You will get the screen in Figure 4.2.

Figure 4.2 *Stroop Task* practice parameters screen.

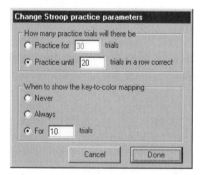

Change Stroop practice parameters

How many practice trials will there be
○ Practice for [30]   trials
● Practice until [20]   trials in a row correct

When to show the key-to-color mapping
○ Never
○ Always
● For [10]   trials

[Cancel]   [Done]

You can present a set number of practice trials, or you can require a certain number of consecutive trials to be correct before the practice will end. You can also have the mapping from key to color on screen during practice. This can always be on, or it can be on for a set number of trials and then go away. Choose practice settings and click "Done."

Setting the presentation parameters   Click the "Change" button by "Presentation Parameters." You will get the screen in Figure 4.3.

Figure 4.3 *Stroop Task* presentation parameters screen.

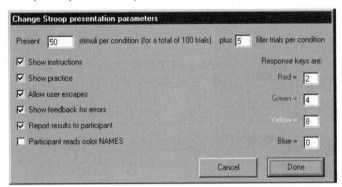

Set the number of trials to present in each condition. The program will randomly choose stimuli from the set of stimuli in the stimulus folder until the total number of trials has been presented. You may also add filler trials to each condition. These trials will look like the real trials but will not be scored. Filler trials allow participants a few practice trials to get their fingers ready before the real experiment starts.

"Show instructions" will present the standard instructions. "Show practice" presents the practice. Checking "Allow user escapes" allows the user to type "q" as a response to terminate the program early. Checking "Show feedback for errors" causes the computer to display "ERROR" whenever the wrong response is selected (the Macintosh version of the program beeps for errors). Checking "Report results to participant" will show the results on screen after the experiment has been presented (the program reports after each block of trials for Macintosh users). Checking "Participant reads color NAMES" will change the instructions to require word reading and not color naming. You will need a set of stimuli that are correctly configured if you choose this option. Finally, choose response keys for participants. The default set was chosen to allow participants' hands to rest comfortably on the keyboard with their fingers on the row of numbers at the top. Click "Done" when you finish setting presentation parameters.

On the main parameters screen, you will see a brief verbal description of all of your parameter settings. If everything looks OK, choose "Save Set-Up File." Name your parameter file and choose a location to save it. Whenever you want to run the experiment you have just set up, double-click your parameter file to launch the program. Click "Done" to return to the main screen. Enter a participant number and run the program to test your parameters. You should always test your parameter settings when you make a new experiment.

■ The *Stroop Analysis* Software

When you finish collecting data, you will need to analyze it using the *Stroop Analysis* software. You can view the results for a single participant or prepare a file with the results of an entire experiment. You will have to run the data files through the analysis program before you will be able to view the results.

❏ *Viewing a Participant's Data File*

To print a single participant's results, double-click that participant's data file. You will see the screen in Figure 4.4.

Figure 4.4 *Stroop Analysis* output parameters screen.

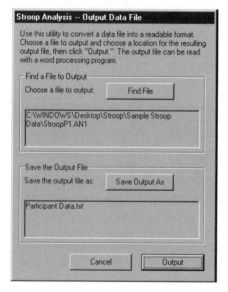

If you double-clicked a data file, you can click "Output" and the data will be processed. The file that is created will be saved in the same folder as the data file and will be called "Participant Data." Double-clicking the output file will allow you to see the results for that participant. If the analysis program is already running, chose "Output Data File" from the main window to get this screen. (Macintosh users will choose actions from the "Analysis Menu" in the menu bar.) Choose "Find File" to choose a file to print. Click "Save Output As" to create a file for the processed data. You will be asked to choose a name and location for the data file. Macintosh users have the option of sending a file to the printer, but this option may not always work correctly.

❏ *Analyzing a Group of Data Files*

If you double-click the *Stroop Analysis* program and choose "Analyze Data" from the main screen, you will see the screen in Figure 4.5. (Macintosh users will choose actions from the "Analysis Menu" in the menu bar.)

Figure 4.5 *Stroop Analysis* analysis parameters screen.

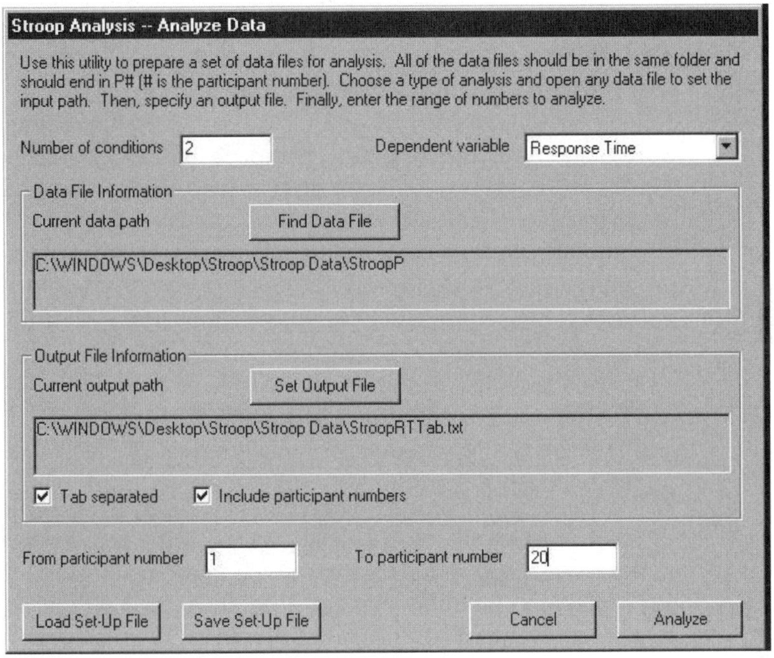

This part of the analysis program will let you analyze the results of multiple data files. To run an analysis, enter the number of conditions from the experiment and choose whether you want to analyze accuracy or response time data. Click the "Find Data File" button and choose any Stroop data file. For the program to work correctly, all data files need to be named "StroopP#" where the "#" is the participant number, and all data files need to be in the same folder. The naming convention will automatically be followed if you use the default name from the main program. You also need to specify where to save the results of the analysis by clicking "Set Output File." (For Macintosh users, a default output path will be created automatically.) Enter a "From" and "To" participant number. Then, click "Analyze." The program will construct a data file with the appropriate dependent measure in each condition for each participant. You can use this data file in any statistics program to compute descriptive and inferential statistics. More information on using the analysis program is available in Appendix B.

Suggested Projects

☆ 1. You can replicate the original Stroop (1935) experiments using the *Stroop Task* software. You can also create stimulus cards to implement a paper-and-pencil version of Stroop's original experiments (this technique is actually closer to Stroop's procedure).

2. You can conduct a number of variations on the Stroop (1935) procedure.

   a. Stroop's (1935) control group in Experiment 2 was colored rectangles. He was able to show that trying to name the colors of color words (written in different colors of ink) was harder than pure color naming. But why is it harder? Is it competition from similar responses (two colors competing against each other)? Or is it a more general competition (a word response competing with a color response)? If you substitute different control groups, you can answer that question and others like it. Some that have been included with the software:

   ☆   i. *Number words in colors.* If wordiness causes the interference, number words should slow performance as much as color words. If it takes a specific form of interference, color words should hurt performance more than number words.

   ☆   ii. *Pseudowords (wred, bloo, yeloe,* and *grene).* It may be the sound of the word that causes the interference, or it may be the visual appearance of the word. These stimuli will let you tell which is causing the interference.

   ☆   iii. *Matching color words.* There will still be two responses, but they will not compete. This will let you tell if the interference is due to two responses or due to a mismatch in the responses.

   ☆   You can probably think of other ideas as well. For each alternative explanation of Stroop interference, you will need to create a new control group. If you are interested in narrowing down how semantic interference operates in the Stroop task, a good experiment to start with was performed by Klein (1964). Klein had six conditions: nonwords (*evjc*); rare words (*abjure*); common words (*put*); words that implicate colors (*lemon*); color words, but different from the response colors (*tan*); and color words in mismatching colors (*red* in blue ink). Klein expected interference to increase as the words got more color-related. This is essentially the pattern shown by his results. So, color words cause the most interference, but common words are also going to cause some interference. You can find additional information on this topic in reviews by Dyer (1973) and MacLeod (1991).

   ☆   b. Strooplike interference can also be shown with number naming. For example, Windes (1968) showed that naming the number of digits presented was harder when the number and the digit mismatched (e.g., "3 3," "2 2 2 2"). How is number Stroop interference related to color Stroop interference? Is it a similar mechanism, or are the two phenomena distinct?

3. The Stroop task has also been used as a tool in clinical assessment. Some examples:

☆☆   a. Kindt and Brosschot (1997) examined the effect of spider pictures and spider words on Stroop interference. They placed pictures of spiders on colored disks and asked people to name the color of the disk. They also wrote spider words in colors (*cobweb*, *spider*) and had participants name the color. For a control group, they chose a set of stimuli that are similar to spiders in shape, but have no negative connotations (pictures of stools and chairs). The results were that spider phobics showed the same amount of interference to threatening words and threatening pictures. Kindt and Brosschot argue that this shows the irrationality of the phobia. An actual spider is more threatening than a word, but phobics reacted in the same way to both in the Stroop task. The spider word stimuli are included with the *Stroop Task* software. If you want to implement the full Kindt and Brosschot experiment, you will need to create the spider picture stimuli.

☆☆☆   b. Cooper and Todd (1997) presented three kinds of eating concern words to participants with anorexia nervosa and bulimia nervosa. The word types were eating words (*diet*), weight words (*pounds*), and shape words (*thighs*). Both groups showed interference for eating and weight words, anorexia nervosa patients also showed interference for shape words. Cooper and Todd interpret this as showing that the Stroop task can discriminate between the two types of disorder.

> **ETHICS NOTE 4.1**   Working with special participant populations raises a number of tricky ethical issues. First, privacy concerns are even more important when the information you are collecting has the potential to be embarrassing or harmful if others find out about it. You will need to take extra precautions to ensure confidentiality and anonymity. Second, there is increased risk of harm when sensitive questions are being asked. You will have a difficult time getting approval to conduct research with special populations, so you will need to plan early and be sure that you have carefully considered the balance between risks and benefits.

   c. Other types of assessment:

☆☆☆   i. Motta, Joseph, Rose, Suozzi, and Leiderman (1997) showed that children of war veterans have Stroop interference for war-related words. They interpret this as showing that the Stroop task can assess the transfer of war experiences from veterans to their children.

☆☆☆   ii. Pincus, Fraser, and Pearce (1998) looked at Stroop interference for chronic pain sufferers. Pain sufferers did not show interference for pain words, suggesting that pain does not produce an attentional bias all by itself.

☆☆☆   iii. Lundh and Radon (1998) looked at Stroop interference as an index of death anxiety. They found that all participants showed interference for death-related words but that the amount of interference correlated with age (the older you are, the more interference).

☆☆☆   iv. Mattia, Heimberg, and Hope (1993) investigated Stroop interference in social phobics. They found that social phobics showed interference to social threat words. This index was able to distinguish between people who respond to treatment for social phobia and people who do not respond to treatment.

☆☆☆ 4. In general, the amount of Stroop interference to various word types can be used to assess what is on a person's mind. As a project, you might try to design a Stroop task to assess some other aspect of psychological functioning. For example, can a Stroop task discriminate between Type A and Type B personalities? One advantage of the Stroop task over other measures is that participants are not generally aware of the manipulation in a Stroop task. So, it is hard for them to fake their responses (or make changes in their responses due to testing). This point was made by Lundh and Radon (1998), who found that religious people and atheists report different amounts of death anxiety but show the same Stroop interference to death words. When stated opinions do not match actual behavior, the Stroop task may be a better way to assess psychological variables.

☆☆ 5. Another use of Stroop would be as the dependent variable for other projects. For example, some of my students used a standard Stroop task to assess the effects of caffeine on performance. They found that caffeine speeds responding without affecting error rates.

■ ■ ■ ■ ■ ■
References

Cooper, M., & Todd, G. (1997). Selective processing of three types of stimuli in eating disorders. *British Journal of Clinical Psychology, 36,* 279–281.

Dyer, F. S. (1973). The Stroop phenomenon and its use in the study of perceptual, cognitive, and response processes. *Memory & Cognition, 1,* 106–120.

Kindt, M., & Brosschot, J. F. (1997). Phobia-related cognitive bias for pictorial and linguistic stimuli. *Journal of Abnormal Psychology, 106,* 644–648.

Klein, G. S. (1964). Semantic power measured through the interference of words with color-naming. *American Journal of Psychology, 77,* 576–588.

Lundh, L. G., & Radon, V. (1998). Death anxiety as a function of belief in an afterlife: A comparison between a questionnaire measure and a Stroop measure of death anxiety. *Personality and Individual Differences, 25,* 487–494.

MacLeod, C. M. (1991). Half a century of research on the Stroop effect: An integrative review. *Psychological Bulletin, 109,* 163–203.

MacLeod, C. M. (1992). The Stroop task: The "gold standard" of attentional measures. *Journal of Experimental Psychology: General, 121,* 12–14.

Mattia, J. I., Heimberg, R. G., & Hope, D. A. (1993). The revised Stroop color-naming task in social phobics. *Behaviour Research and Therapy, 31,* 305–313.

Motta, R. W., Joseph, J. M., Rose, R. D., Suozzi, J. M., & Leiderman, L. J. (1997). Secondary trauma: Assessing intergenerational transmission of war experiences with a modified Stroop procedure. *Journal of Clinical Psychology, 53,* 895–903.

Pincus, T., Fraser, L., & Pearce, S. (1998). Do chronic pain patients "Stroop" on pain stimuli? *British Journal of Clinical Psychology, 37,* 49–58.

Stroop, J. R. (1935). Studies of interference in serial verbal reactions. *Journal of Experimental Psychology, 18,* 643–662.

Windes, J. D. (1968). Reaction time for numerical coding and naming of numerals. *Journal of Experimental Psychology, 78,* 318–322.

One-Way Designs I

I can't think when I'm sitting on my hands

Why do people gesture when they talk? A recent idea is that speakers gesture because it helps them think of what to say. In other words, gestures are as much for the speaker's benefit as for the listener's benefit. The target article for this chapter (Frick-Horbury & Guttentag, 1998) looked at how the ability to gesture helps people retrieve words when given the definition (for example, what word is defined as "a flexible, threadlike, incandescent object inside a lightbulb"?). Some participants retrieved words while holding a rod (restricted), and others were free to move their hands (unrestricted). The unrestricted participants thought of more words given the definition and remembered more of the words later.

■ ■ ■ ■ ■

Introduction: Experiments with More than Two Groups and One Independent Variable

Sometimes, you will want to include more than two groups in your experimental design. For example, in the basic Stroop experiment in Chapter 4, there were only two groups: color words (written in different colors than the color named by the word) and colored boxes. When people name the colors of these two kinds of stimuli, they take longer for the words than the boxes. Stroop's explanation was that the meaning of the color word competes with the name of the color, making people slower to respond. Let's consider an additional question about this response competition. Is it the fact that the words are color words that makes people slower, or will people slow down for *any* word, no matter what it names?

To answer this question, we need a third kind of stimulus (and a third group in the experiment). These stimuli need to be noncolor words written in the same colors as the color words. For instance, we could use the number words *one*, *two*, *three*, and *four* written in red, green, yellow, and blue. If we have people name the colors of these noncolor words, we can find out if simply looking at a word produces the interference or if it is the fact that the words name colors that produces the interference.

One thing to note about our new design with three groups is that all three still comprise the levels (or conditions) of one independent variable. You can tell this because they all line up on a single dimension. In this case, the dimension would be something like "amount of response competition." At one end are the color words, in the middle are the number words, and at the other end are the boxes. As you move from one end to the other, the thing that changes is the extent to which the item produces response competition. All of the designs in this chapter and in Chapter 6 have this property. There will always be more than two groups but only one independent variable. We will call these **one-way designs** because there is only one independent variable (only one thing being manipulated). As long as there is only one independent variable, you can have as many groups within that variable as you would like and still have a one-way design. In Chapters 7 and 8, we will consider designs with more than one independent variable.

Why do researchers use one-way designs with more than two groups? There are two main reasons:

1. *To include all of the required control groups (or all of the required groups).* As we discussed in Chapter 4, coming up with the appropriate comparison group can be difficult. Think about the Stroop experiment again. Each of the following control groups could be used to understand some aspect of the interference that causes people to slow down when they name the colors of color words.

   a. Colored rectangles.
   b. Number words.
   c. Pseudoword homophones (letter strings that are not words, but sound like color words, such as *bloo*).
   d. Color words written in the color that they name (like *red* in red).

We have already discussed the first two. Pseudowords could tell us if it is the visual appearance of the word that interferes or if it is the sound of the word (because they all sound like color words but do not look like color words). Color words written in the color named could tell us if the interference comes from simultaneously processing two sorts of information (words and colors) or if it is due to response competition (trying to choose between two types of responses). If it is the former, people should be slow even when the words match the color. If it is response competition, people should be fast in this condition.

We could do four separate two group experiments to answer these questions, but that would waste time, and it would also rule out certain comparisons (like number words vs. pseudowords). Instead, we would do one big experiment with five kinds of stimuli.

2. Another reason to use one-way designs with more than two groups is to deal with a problem called **restriction of range**. This occurs when the groups

you have chosen do not adequately cover the appropriate values of the independent variable. How do researchers know how many groups to include? One approach is to include enough conditions to fully cover the potential range of the independent variable, even though some of them are probably more extreme than necessary. When extensive research has been done in an area, it is possible to survey the literature to find out how many conditions to include.

Our target article for this chapter used a one-way design (I am simplifying some aspects of their design). We will look at the effect of hand gestures on the retrieval of word meanings. The basic question is this: How well can people retrieve words when they cannot move their hands?

■■■■■■
Target Article: Gesture and Thought

Why do people gesture when they talk? Your first response to this question might be: to help the person to whom they are talking understand what they mean. That is a good idea, and plenty of research supports that conclusion, but it is not the whole story. Why do I say this? First, some evidence shows that people gesture even when the person they are talking to cannot see them (Rimé, 1982). For example, people gesture when they are talking on the telephone. They cannot expect those gestures to help the person on the other end of the line understand what they are saying.

Another line of research showing that gesture is not just for the listener was provided by Iverson and Goldin-Meadow (1998; see also Iverson & Goldin-Meadow, 1997). They studied the gestures of people who were blind from birth. In Iverson and Goldin-Meadow's research, blind people gestured just as much as sighted people (around 1.5 gestures per task in their experiment). Interestingly, blind people produced as many gestures talking to another blind person as they produced talking to a sighted person.

So, people gesture even when the listener cannot take advantage of the information. Why do it? One hypothesis is that it helps people retrieve the words they want to say. For example, if you are trying to think of *ukulele*, it may help to pantomime playing a ukulele. This hypothesis was tested by the authors of the target article for this chapter.

Frick-Horbury and Guttentag (1998) restricted people's hand movements and asked them to think of words when given a definition. For example, what word is defined by "an arch or hoop in croquet that balls have to be hit through"? (The answer is *wicket*.) Their hypothesis was simple: People who cannot gesture should have a harder time retrieving the words.

Experiment 1

For the first experiment, there were two gesture groups (in the projects section I will suggest designs that have more than two groups). The first group was unrestricted; these participants could do whatever they wanted with their hands (their foot was on a pedal to make all participants adopt the same posture). The second group was restricted; they held a rod in their hands that prevented them from gesturing.

Both groups tried to retrieve the words for 50 definitions (see the chapter supplement for the definitions). Participants had as much as one minute to think of the word. If they did not know, they could move along faster than that.

The results were clear. People successfully retrieved more words when they could gesture (23.6 words) than when they were restricted (18.7 words). After the test, participants were asked to recall as many of the words as they could. Unrestricted participants could also recall more of the words (16.8 words) than restricted participants (11.0 words). So, gesturing seems to improve word retrieval and memory for the words.

Another interesting result was found by looking at the gestures produced in the unrestricted group. There was no relationship between gesturing and retrieval. In other words, people were just as likely to retrieve a word when they made a gesture as when they did not make a gesture. Frick-Horbury and Guttentag (1998) hypothesize that it may be *imagined* gestures that make the difference, and gesture imagery is what is interfered with when participants hold the rod (Saltz & Donnenwerth-Nolan, 1981, found that imagining motor movements can improve retention, suggesting a role for gesture imagery). We will take up this issue again in the projects section.

Experiment 2

Experiment 2 was a replication of Experiment 1. The only difference was in the kind of restriction. Frick-Horbury and Guttentag (1998) were worried that holding the bar may have caused stress for participants, distracting them from the task of retrieving word meanings. What you are doing with your hands can have an effect on cognition. For example, Berkowitz and Troccoli (1990) showed that holding your arm in an uncomfortable position can negatively impact ratings of a person. To counteract this effect, Frick-Horbury and Guttentag had participants hold their hands in the pockets of an apron. Participants' movements were restricted, but the pocket restriction was more natural. These participants were similar to the restricted participants in Experiment 1 (18.8 words retrieved, 9.4 words recalled). The effect in Experiment 1 probably was not due to stress caused by holding the rod.

■ ■ ■ ■ ■ ■
Implementing the Design

Materials

1. The list of definitions used by Frick-Horbury and Guttentag (1998) is in the chapter supplement. Their rules for choosing these words are also summarized in the chapter supplement, and you could use these rules to construct your own lists.

2. If you want to try to analyze the actual gestures people produce (which will be a *very* difficult task), you will need a video camera. You will probably not be able to code the gestures using a regular VCR. If someone at your school does research on behavior and regularly videotapes participants, you may be able to borrow their equipment or lab space for your project. Do not undertake a gesture coding experiment lightly. Seek the advice of people who code behavior on video and make sure you do everything you can to get data that you can score later.

For a specific coding scheme (and a very comprehensive summary of gesture research), I suggest reading David McNeill's book *Hand and Mind: What Gestures Reveal about Thought*. Try to figure out how you will score the data before you collect it.

Suggested Projects

☆ 1. You can replicate the Frick-Horbury and Guttentag (1998) experiments using the word list in the chapter supplement. The simple version of this project would be to essentially ignore the gestures produced by the unrestricted group. Students in my class have gotten by with counting the number of gestures produced for each word retrieval. You will lose a lot of information, but practical matters do come into play.

2. You can conduct a number of variations on the Frick-Horbury and Guttentag (1998) procedure.

☆☆ a. Why is there no relationship between gesturing and retrieval for the unrestricted group? Frick-Horbury and Guttentag (1998) hypothesize that it is not *actual* gestures that make a difference, it is the ability to imagine gestures that helps retrieval. One way to test this would be to add a restricted-informed group (some of my students have tried this). This group is told that they are holding the rod to prevent them from gesturing. The idea is that calling attention to their inability to physically gesture may encourage them to use gesture imagery instead, making them more like the unrestricted group.

☆☆☆ b. You could also interfere with gesture imagery explicitly. Saltz and Donnenwerth-Nolan (1981) interfered with gesture imagery by using a visual interference task. Participants read sentences like "quickly the grandmother stomped the spider" and they were instructed to imagine the action in the sentence. For interference, they were shown a picture (e.g., an artist painting a self-portrait), and they were to get a mental image of this picture. The visual interference of imagining the picture interfered with memory for the sentences. This suggests the manipulation for our project. You could have an unrestricted group, a restricted group, and a visual interference group (who do a task like those in Saltz and Donnenwerth-Nolan). If the visual interference group matches the restricted group, it would lend support to the idea that imagined gestures improve retrieval. You could also try other tasks to interfere with gesture imagery. Guilford (1967) may be a good place to look for some interference tasks.

In his studies on working memory, Baddeley (1986) uses a task called "articulatory suppression" to interfere with verbal memory. Basically, a person says "the, the, the . . ." while performing a task. Using the articulators interferes with memory. You might try a similar "gestural suppression" task. Have the participants flap their hands to interfere with gesture imagery.

   c. You could try variations on the word lists. Basically, what kinds of verbal information are affected by restriction? Some thoughts:

☆☆   i. *Easier words.* What will restriction do when the words are more common (higher frequency of use in the language)? Maybe gesture is only important for the hard ones. You could have a restricted group with three levels of frequency (e.g., high frequency, medium frequency, low frequency).

☆☆   ii. *Concrete words (imageable words, etc.).* Paivio, Yuille, and Madigan (1968) list concreteness, imageableness, and meaningfulness ratings for 925 nouns. You could compare restriction on different levels of each of these variables. For example, have high-, medium-, and low-imagery words in a restricted condition. Are all words equally affected by restriction, or just certain ones? For example, if gesture imagery is the key factor, you might think high-imagery words (*dog*) would be more affected than low imagery words (*truth*).

☆☆☆   iii. *Gesture/action verbs.* Find a list of words that imply an action (*swing, tickle,* etc.). How does restriction affect verb retrieval as you go from physical action (*throw*) to intermediate (*think*) to no physical action (*solve*)? You should probably consult a word-norming study to find out how much physical action is associated with particular verbs.

☆☆☆   d. Are there other aspects of language production besides word retrieval that would be affected by gesture? For example, gesture may be like priming the pump for cognitive activity. It is not really activating the meaning of any particular words, just moving along the thinking process. You would have to do some library research to find out what other people have proposed (McNeill, 1992, would be a good source for ideas).

☆☆☆   e. Frick-Horbury and Guttentag (1998) were concerned about the task they used to restrict gesturing. They had two different tasks: holding a rod and hands in pocket. Does the type of restriction affect retrieval? You could add additional levels of restriction to their design. For example, some restrictions might call attention to a person's hands, and others might not. You could vary restriction methods along this "attention to hands" dimension.

Another alternative would be to incorporate stress into the restriction so you can explicitly find out about the effects of stress on retrieval.

Berkowitz and Troccoli (1990) had people hold their arms straight out from their sides for two minutes. This appeared to produce stress in participants. You could include a condition like this as one restricted condition. At the other end of the stress dimension would be hands comfortably held in pockets. You could have other conditions in-between. Frick-Horbury and Guttentag (1998) concluded that their results were not due to stress, with an explicit test you can find out if that is true.

3. Although it is not really in keeping with the spirit of the target article, you could look at the effect of gesture on the listener. Krauss, Dushay, Chen, and Rauscher (1995) manipulated the extent to which a listener could take advantage of gestures. People were videotaped describing objects to be manipulated. Some listeners saw these tapes and heard the soundtrack. Others heard the soundtrack but could not see the gestures. People did not do better when they could see the gestures. Krauss et al. took this to mean that the gestures are not really intended to help the listener. This experiment suggests a couple of projects.

☆☆☆   a. There is at least one more level that could be included here: gestures but not soundtrack. What would happen if the person could see but not hear the speaker? Will the gestures alone allow a listener to pick out the right objects?

☆☆☆   b. Clark has worked out the way that "common ground" influences conversation (e.g., Clark, Schreuder, & Buttrick, 1983). Basically, as people establish a set of shared assumptions in a conversation, the information they can convey changes (see project 6b below for an example of common ground and gesturing). People who watch a speaker gesture for a different listener have not had an opportunity to establish common ground with the speaker. Maybe this accounts for the findings of Krauss et al. (1995). In other words, gestures will improve comprehension but only for listeners who have established common ground with the speaker. Could you incorporate common ground in the design used by Krauss et al.? One way might be to have a speaker and listener interact for enough trials to establish common ground, then videotape the speaker on some new trials and see if gesture adds anything to comprehension. For this project, you would need to do some background reading on how common ground is established in conversation.

4. There are other general gesture projects not really related to the target article that do involve gesture.

☆☆☆   a. One factor in conversation is something called "audience design." People tend to tailor their message to the person they are speaking to. Assumptions about the listener's background knowledge and cognitive ability come into play. For example, you would probably explain the death of a close relative to a small child differently than to an adult sibling.

How will gesturing be affected by audience design? Some students in my cognitive science class tackled this as a lab project. They chose three passages from a physics book (Mercury's perihelion shift, Einstein's theory of relativity, and how the moon causes tides). Participants read these until they fully understood the passage. Then, they explained the passage to a hypothetical other. The three audiences were a four-year-old child, a fellow student, and a physics professor. We hypothesized that there would be more gesturing when speaking to a child than to a physics professor. I would like to tell you about the results here, but that is where the project bogged down. All of the cautionary notes above about the difficulty of coding gestures were based on personal experience. It is *very* hard to code all of the gestures in a three-minute speech. We did perform a rough count of the number of gestures, and there were more for the child than the professor. Analysis of the various types of gestures will have to wait until some ambitious students with about 3,000 hours on their hands are willing to take on the coding. Keeping in mind the difficulty involved in coding gesture, some incorporation of audience design may still be possible.

☆☆☆   b. How is gesturing affected by common ground? Clark et al. (1983) manipulated common ground and looked at its impact on the interpretation of "demonstrative references" (references that include a gesture as an essential component). For example, imagine that you are holding a newspaper and someone asks, "Can I have that paper?" pointing to the paper. In the newspaper example, the target of the gesture is pretty clear. But suppose there are four flowers in a picture and I ask you, "What color is this flower?" How will you decide what to say? The more common ground we share (the more we both know about the situation), the easier it will be to answer.

In one experiment, Clark et al. (1983) looked at people's interpretation of ambiguous demonstrative references based on various amounts of common ground. To manipulate common ground, the experimenters said they were choosing a present for a conservative uncle or a modern cousin. Then they asked people, "What do you think of this?" with an array of objects (like four watches). The common ground (whom the gift was for) influenced people's interpretation of "this." As a project, you might investigate the effect of common ground on people's gesturing. For example, do friends gesture as much as strangers when they are communicating? Will strangers viewing a tape of friends talking be able to interpret the gestures, or do people create their own gestures based on common ground?

■ ■ ■ ■ ■ ■
References

Baddeley, A. (1986). *Working memory.* Oxford, U.K.: Oxford University Press.

Berkowitz, L., & Troccoli, B. T. (1990). Feelings, direction of attention, and expressed evaluations of others. *Cognition and Emotion, 4,* 305–325.

Clark, H. H., Schreuder, R., & Buttrick, S. (1983). Common ground and the understanding of demonstrative reference. *Journal of Verbal Learning and Verbal Behavior, 22,* 245–258.

Frick-Horbury, D., & Guttentag, R. E. (1998). The effects of restricting hand gesture production on lexical retrieval and free recall. *American Journal of Psychology, 111,* 43–62.

Guilford, J. P. (1967). *The nature of human intelligence.* New York: McGraw-Hill.

Iverson, J. M., & Goldin-Meadow, S. (1997). What's communication got to do with it? Gesture in children blind from birth. *Developmental Psychology, 33,* 453–467.

Iverson, J. M., & Goldin-Meadow, S. (1998). Why people gesture when they speak. *Nature, 396,* 228.

Krauss, R. M., Dushay, R. A., Chen, Y., & Rauscher, F. (1995). The communicative value of conversational hand gestures. *Journal of Experimental Social Psychology, 31,* 533–552.

McNeill, D. (1992). *Hand and mind: What gestures reveal about thought.* Chicago: University of Chicago Press.

Paivio, A., Yuille, J. C., & Madigan, S. (1968). Concreteness, imagery, and meaningfulness values for 925 nouns. *Journal of Experimental Psychology Monographs, 76* (1, Pt. 2).

Rimé, B. (1982). The elimination of visible behaviour from social interactions: The effect on verbal, nonverbal, and interpersonal variables. *European Journal of Social Psychology, 12,* 113–129.

Saltz, E., & Donnenwerth-Nolan, S. (1981). Does motoric imagery facilitate memory for sentences? A selective interference test. *Journal of Verbal Learning and Verbal Behavior, 20,* 322–332.

Words and Definitions from Frick-Horbury and Guttentag (1998)

1. *Mannequin:* A lifelike model of a human figure used to display clothing in a shop window.
2. *Hieroglyphics:* A picture script of the ancient Egyptian people usually carved on the stones in pyramids.
3. *Guillotine:* An ancient machine for beheading by means of a heavy blade.
4. *Skewer:* A piece of thin metal used to pierce and cook a beef kabob over an open fire.
5. *Kaleidoscope:* An instrument containing loose bits of colored glass that produce an ever-changing pattern when the position is revolved.
6. *Lasso:* A long rope with a running noose that is used for roping cows and horses.
7. *Chaps:* Leather leggings resembling trousers without a seat that are usually worn by cowboys.
8. *Buoy:* A floating object moored to the bottom of a body of water to mark a channel.
9. *Loupe:* A small, magnifying eyepiece used by jewelers and watchmakers.
10. *Kamikaze:* A Japanese air attack corps assigned to make suicidal crashes on a target.
11. *Wicket:* An arch or hoop in croquet that the balls have to be hit through.
12. *Horizontal:* A word used for the position of an object that is parallel to the plane of the ground.
13. *Machete:* A large, heavy knife used for cutting a path through the jungle.
14. *Javelin:* A slender shaft of wood tipped with iron and thrown for distance in an athletic field event.
15. *Ukulele:* A very small guitar with four strings popularized by Hawaiian musicians.
16. *Trellis:* A frame of latticework for climbing plants in a yard.
17. *Skylight:* An opening in a house roof to admit sunshine.
18. *Palette:* A thin, oval tablet with a hole for the thumb at one end by which a painter holds it and mixes different shades of pigment on it.
19. *Silhouette:* A black cutout of paper to represent the outline of a person's head.
20. *Gargoyle:* A carved, grotesque human or animal figure projecting from the roof of a building, typical of older structures, especially castles.
21. *Castanets:* A small rhythm instrument used especially by dancers, consisting of two small shells that are clicked together by the fingers.
22. *Metronome:* A pendulum-like instrument designed to mark exact time by a regular ticking, such as 2/4 time for a piano score.
23. *Atomizer:* The name of a type of perfume container which typically sprays a fine mist when the air bulb is squeezed.

24. *Bellows:* A tool-like object with accordion pleats that blows air out of one end and is used to intensify a fire.
25. *Banister:* A handrail usually going down a staircase, made of smooth, rounded wood with perpendicular supports adjoining to the stairs.
26. *Tambourine:* A one-sided drum with loose metallic disks in the sides that is played by shaking.
27. *Chandelier:* A large, ornate lighting fixture hanging from the ceiling.
28. *Monocle:* An eyeglass for one eye held in place by the lower eye socket and upper eye lid.
29. *Tuning fork:* A two-pronged, metal instrument that gives a fixed, pure tone when struck.
30. *Abacus:* An ancient instrument for performing calculations by sliding disks along a series of straight rods.
31. *Bleachers:* Uncovered stand of progressively higher rows of wooden planks for spectators to sit on.
32. *Curtsy:* An action showing respect to royalty, usually performed by women, where they bow slightly and bend at the knee.
33. *Escargot:* A garden snail eaten as an appetizer.
34. *Filament:* A flexible, threadlike, incandescent object inside a light bulb.
35. *Washboard:* A corrugated, rectangular surface women used to use to scrub clothes.
36. *Gondola:* A long, narrow, flat-bottomed boat used in the canals of Venice.
37. *Matador:* The name used for a person that fights bulls.
38. *Iguana:* The name of a large lizard with a serrated dorsal crest, found in the tropical regions of South America.
39. *Rheostat:* A type of light switch that dims or brightens a lighting fixture.
40. *Shamrock:* A cloverlike plant typically used as a symbolic emblem by the Irish and thought to be good luck.
41. *Harpoon:* A large, barbed spear used for hunting whale or other large fish.
42. *Labyrinth:* A large maze usually defined by tall shrubbery.
43. *Kiln:* A large oven used to fire clay or ceramic pottery.
44. *Urn:* A type of vase used to store the cremated remains of a person.
45. *Eclair:* A type of pastry with a cream-filled center, covered with chocolate.
46. *Scarab:* An Egyptian stone ornament in the shape of a beetle.
47. *Syringe:* A needle device used to give an injection to a person.
48. *Bassinet:* A type of cradle used for infants, made of wicker with a hood over one end.
49. *Gyroscope:* A toy or instrument used to illustrate Earth's rotation by balancing and spinning rapidly about an axis.
50. *Plurality:* A number consisting of more than one, a majority.

Words were chosen via the following procedure:

1. Words were all English names of common objects or concepts.
2. Words were low in frequency (essentially, the number of times they appear in print per million words). You should consult a word frequency book to check word frequency [such as Kuçera, H., & Francis, W. N. (1967). *Computational analysis of present-day American English.* Providence, RI: Brown University Press].
3. The words were tested on a group of people to make sure they produced TOT states around 10% of the time.
4. There were only 49 words in the Appendix to the original article, so I selected number 50 out of my *Buster Brown Webster Selected Dictionary* (1923).

Source: From "The effects of restricting hand gesture production on lexical retrieval and free recall," by D. Frick-Horbury and R. E. Guttentag, 1998, *American Journal of Psychology, 111,* pp. 43–62. Copyright © 1998 by the Board of Trustees of the University of Illinois. Used with the permission of the University of Illinois Press and the author.

6

One-Way Designs II

In a blue room with red curtains

Does the color of the environment have an effect on people? That was the question for our target article for this chapter (Nakshian, 1964). Participants performed nine tasks in either a red, green, or gray environment. The tasks were designed to test a theory that red produces arousal and attention to external events, whereas green produces a more tranquil state that leaves people less influenced by external events. The results were mixed. There was a difference for two motor tasks (e.g., more hand tremor in a red environment). For seven of the tasks, there were no differences due to color.

■ ■ ■ ■ ■ ■
Introduction: Experiments with More than Two Groups and One Independent Variable

The target article for this chapter uses a one-way design with more than two groups. These designs were discussed at length in the opening section of Chapter 5. If you have not already done so, you may want to read that before continuing here.

■ ■ ■ ■ ■ ■
Target Article: Room Color and Mood

A number of environmental factors have been shown to have a negative effect on people (see Baum, Aiello, & Calesnick, 1978, for the effects of crowding; Staples, 1996, for the effect of environmental noise; and Knez, 1995, for the effect of office lighting). Can the color of the environment also have negative effects? The same sorts of variables affected by other environmental factors could also be affected by color (such as mood, productivity, or performance). As Ainsworth, Simpson, and Cassell (1993) point out, the answer to this question is important if productivity is affected by color. To maximize performance, the interior design of offices would need to be planned for the work to be performed in the space. Indirect savings are also possible if there is a relationship between the color of lighting and thermal comfort. Fanger, Breum, and Jerking (1977) note that "warmer" light could lower heating costs in the winter and "cooler" light could lower air conditioning costs in the summer. The target article for this chapter investigates the effects of color on various aspects of performance.

There seems to be some consensus that warm colors are more arousing than cool colors when physiological arousal is measured. O'Connell, Harper, and McAndrew (1985) found that men's grip strength is higher when staring at a red wall than when staring at a green wall. Hamid and Newport (1989) also found that children's grip strength was higher in a pink room than in a blue room. Wilson (1966) found that galvanic skin response (GSR) was higher when staring at a red slide than at a green slide, suggesting that red is more arousing.

When mood is the dependent measure, the situation is a little more complex. Hamid and Newport (1989) found more positive mood drawings in a pink environment than in a blue environment. Jacobs and Suess (1975) found that yellow and red produce more anxiety than green and blue. Kwallek, Lewis, and Robbins (1988) and Ainsworth et al. (1993), on the other hand, found no effect of red and blue on mood.

Our target article for this chapter was designed to test a general theory of the effects of color on humans. The theory was developed by Goldstein (e.g., Goldstein, 1942, cited in Nakshian, 1964) based on his experiences with brain-damaged participants. Nakshian describes several of Goldstein's experiments. The basic findings were that people spread their arms farther apart when staring at red than when staring at green; people move their arms away from their body at a faster rate when staring at red and toward their bodies at a faster rate when staring at green; and that some psychophysical measures are less accurate in red environments than in green environments. These results led Goldstein to propose that red is an "expansive" color that causes people to attend more to the external environment. Red also causes more stimulation or arousal. Green is a "contractive" color that causes introspective states. Because of the different properties of the colors, red should make it hard to focus on judgment or concentration tasks, while green should improve performance on judgment and concentration tasks.

Nakshian (1964) developed several hypotheses from this theory. First, tasks requiring fine motor control will be worse in red environments than in green environments (hypothesis I). Second, performance in tasks requiring psychophysical judgment will be worse in red environments than in green environments (hypothesis II). Third, red will be expansive and green will be contractive (hypothesis III). To test these, Nakshian developed nine tasks.

For hypothesis I, Nakshian (1964) had participants demonstrate hand tremor by trying to keep a stylus in the center of a small hole in a metal plate. Every time the stylus touched the edges of the hole, the time was recorded. Total time of contact with the edges of the hole measured tremor. He also measured tweezer dexterity by having participants use tweezers to pick up small items and place them in holes. Finally, he had participants trace an arc (moving as slowly as possible, but constantly moving). He expected hand movements to be faster in red than green environments.

For hypothesis II, Nakshian (1964) had participants judge line lengths. He also had them estimate five-second time intervals. He expected judgments to be worse in red than in green environments.

For hypothesis III, Nakshian (1964) had participants spread their arms out to a position they found comfortable. He also had them try to spread their arms until they were exactly 10 inches apart. Finally, he had them move their arms inward toward their bodies and outward away from their bodies. He thought that red environments should produce more spread than green environments and also faster outward movement, while green environments should produce faster inward movement.

All of the tasks were performed in a chamber that was completely colored in the appropriate testing color. The walls were made of movable panels that could be easily switched. The floor, table surface, and apparatus were also covered in the color for testing. The independent variable was the color of the chamber. Nakshian (1964) used a red environment, a green environment, and a gray environment (as a control group). So, he had a one-way design with three levels of the independent variable. There were nine dependent variables (performance in each of the tasks described above).

The only significant differences in the results were for the hand tremor and arc tracing tasks. For hand tremor, people were significantly worse in a red environment ($M = 2.82$ seconds of contact) than a green environment ($M = 2.16$ seconds of contact). Neither differed from a gray environment ($M = 2.43$ seconds of contact). For arc tracing, people moved faster in a red environment ($M = 85.07$ seconds) than in a green environment ($M = 98.70$ seconds). Neither differed from a gray environment ($M = 95.12$ seconds). There were no differences in any of the other tasks. These results support one aspect of Goldstein's (1942) theory and also suggest how color may affect worker performance. Any tasks requiring fine motor control should probably not be performed in a red room.

■ ■ ■ ■ ■ ■
Implementing the Design

Materials

The main trick in carrying out this research is to get the rooms colored. If you can get permission to do it, you can paint a room whatever color you need for your experiment. A simpler alternative is to find rooms that are already the color you need. Most college campuses probably have a blue or green classroom somewhere. Red rooms may be harder to come by.

If painting a room is not an option, you can also try to create a special chamber. Make a simple frame and paint some cardboard sheets in the colors you want. Have the participants sit in this chamber (this is similar to Nakshian's 1964 methodology). To change colors, simply switch the cardboard "walls."

Jacobs and Suess (1975) projected the colors onto a wall using a slide projector. You could mimic this procedure, but the entire environment will not be colored. That may affect the results. Another possibility is to get some can lights that sit on the floor. Put high-wattage bulbs in the lights and then place colored gels over the tops of the cans. The lights will bathe the walls of a white room in the appropriate color. You need to be careful not to start a fire using this method.

Finally, Rosenstein (1985) manipulated the color of the environment by draping the walls in fabric. He used medium blue, bright red, bright yellow, and neutral fabrics. You can probably buy cheap fabric in any color you need.

Suggested Projects

A word of caution: Even a casual survey of the color literature will reveal a startling lack of differences attributable to color. There may actually be some small color effect; but, if there is, it will be very hard to find. I have had several groups of students take on color projects, and the experience has always been trying. I have included this topic in the book because it presents a great challenge to any research methods student. If you choose to carry out a confirmation design to show that color is exerting an influence on some aspect of behavior, you will have to use every bit of your research ability to maximize internal validity and minimize error. One suggestion that may be worth considering is to try the strong inference approach (discussed in Chapter 10). Instead of trying to support a hypothesis about the effect of color on behavior, see what hypotheses you can rule out. Pit a color hypothesis against some other hypothesis and design an experiment to test between them.

☆☆ 1. You can replicate Nakshian's (1964) experiment. You will probably not want to use all nine dependent variables.

2. You can vary Nakshian's (1964) basic methodology. Some suggestions:

Changes to Dependent Variables

☆☆   a. Kwallek et al. (1988) and Ainsworth et al. (1993) found no effect of red and blue on typing. This in spite of the fact that typing seems on the surface to be the kind of motor skill that Nakshian's (1964) results suggest would be affected. Can you think of other natural motor tasks that might be affected?

☆☆☆   b. Jacobs and Suess (1975) found that yellow and red produce more anxiety than blue and green, but Kwallek et al. (1988) and Ainsworth et al. (1993) found no effect of color on mood (including scales for depression, anxiety, and arousal). Why might that be? Can you find a mood instrument that might be sensitive enough to detect a change in mood due to color?

☆☆☆   c. Hamid and Newport (1989) used a more indirect measure of mood to find a difference due to color. They had children draw a picture and scored the emotional content of the pictures. Can you think of other indirect mood measures?

☆☆   d. The Stroop task (Chapter 4) can be used as an index of current psychological states. Perhaps it will be sensitive to the arousal caused by red. You might compare people's Stroop interference for arousal words in red, neutral, and green environments.

☆☆☆   e. You might look for other physiological arousal measures. Wilson (1966) showed arousal using GSR. Hooke, Youell, and Etkin (1975) included pulse and blood pressure.

Changes to Independent Variables

☆☆☆   f. The colors may matter. Wilson (1966) proposes that there may be a U-shaped arousal function due to color. Colors at the ends of the spectrum are "dangerous" and cause arousal (red and violet). Colors in the middle are safer and cause less arousal. You already have data from red and green (Wilson). Violet also causes more arousal than green (Nourse & Welch, 1971). Your experiment can include more levels of color (perhaps the entire ROY G BIV spectrum) and determine the arousal function for the various colors.

☆☆☆   g. In an investigation of the tints of office lighting on mood, Knez and Enmarker (1998) found some gender differences. Even though gender is not a true independent variable, it may be interesting to include it in your study. Do men and women show similar arousal effects due to warm colors?

3. You could try alternative means of delivering the colors. Three ideas:

☆☆☆   a. Manipulate the color of the paper that a test is written on. Jacobs and Blandino (1992) presented surveys on blue, green, canary, red, and white paper. They measured several dimensions of mood. The only significant difference was between red and green on the fatigue scale (red was lowest, and green was highest). Herbst and Lester (1995) printed a depression index on blue and white paper. There was no difference in depression scores based on the color of the paper. Are the physiological effects reported above strong enough to affect performance based on the color of the paper a test is printed on? Will this effect apply to some tasks more than others?

☆☆☆   b. You could manipulate color by changing the background color of the screen on a computer monitor. You could measure typing speed and number of errors when using standard background colors vs. other colors. According to Wilson (1966), colors that are more extreme on the spectrum should produce more difficulty.

☆☆☆   c. You have probably heard the expression "seeing life through rose-colored glasses." The normal meaning is that rose-colored glasses make things look better. Can rose-colored glasses make a person more anxious than green glasses would? This would be a relatively simple way to expose a person to a colored environment.

■ ■ ■ ■ ■ ■

References

Ainsworth, R. A., Simpson, L., & Cassell, D. (1993). Effects of three colors in an office interior on mood and performance. *Perceptual and Motor Skills, 76,* 235–241.

Baum, A., Aiello, J. R., & Calesnick, L. E. (1978). Crowding and personal control: Social density and the development of learned helplessness. *Journal of Personality and Social Psychology, 36,* 1000–1011.

Fanger, P. O., Breum, N. O., & Jerking, E. (1977). Can colour and noise influence man's thermal comfort? *Ergonomics, 20,* 11–18.

Goldstein, K. (1942). Some experimental observations concerning the influence of colors on the function of the organism. *Occupational Therapy, 21,* 147–151.

Hamid, P. N., & Newport, A. G. (1989). Effect of colour on physical strength and mood in children. *Perceptual and Motor Skills, 69,* 179–185.

Herbst, A., & Lester, D. (1995). Blue questionnaires and blue mood. *Perceptual and Motor Skills, 81,* 514.

Hooke, J. F., Youell, K. J., & Etkin, M. W. (1975). Color preference and arousal. *Perceptual and Motor Skills, 40,* 710.

Jacobs, K. W., & Blandino, S. E. (1992). Effects of color of paper on which the profile of mood states is printed on the psychological states it measures. *Perceptual and Motor Skills, 75,* 267–271.

Jacobs, K. W., & Suess, J. F. (1975). Effects of four psychological primary colors on anxiety state. *Perceptual and Motor Skills, 41,* 207–210.

Knez, I. (1995). Effects of indoor lighting on mood and cognition. *Journal of Environmental Psychology, 15,* 39–51.

Knez, I., & Enmarker, I. (1998). Effects of office lighting on mood and cognitive performance and a gender effect in work-related judgment. *Environment and Behavior, 30,* 553–567.

Kwallek, N., Lewis, C. M., & Robbins, A. S. (1988). Effects of office interior color on workers' mood and productivity. *Perceptual and Motor Skills, 66,* 123–128.

Nakshian, J. S. (1964). The effects of red and green surroundings on behavior. *The Journal of General Psychology, 70,* 143–161.

Nourse, J. C., & Welch, R. B. (1971). Emotional attributes of color: A comparison of violet and green. *Perceptual and Motor Skills, 32,* 403–406.

O'Connell, B. J., Harper, R. S., & McAndrew, F. T. (1985). Grip strength as a function of exposure to red or green visual stimulation. *Perceptual and Motor Skills, 61,* 1157–1158.

Rosenstein, L. D. (1985). Effect of color of the environment on task performance and mood of males and females with high or low scores on the scholastic aptitude test. *Perceptual and Motor Skills, 60,* 550.

Staples, S. L. (1996). Human response to environmental noise: Psychological research and public policy. *American Psychologist, 51,* 143–150.

Wilson, G. D. (1966). Arousal properties of red versus green. *Perceptual and Motor Skills, 23,* 947–949

Factorial Designs I

Sad sees as sad is

Will a person's mood influence his or her perception of the world? For example, will being in a sad mood cause a person to focus more on sad information than happy information? The authors of our target article for this chapter (Niedenthal and Setterlund, 1994) used classical music to manipulate people's moods and then had them make judgments about words. They found that mood was indeed related to word perception. Words that specifically matched a person's mood were perceived more rapidly.

■ ■ ■ ■ ■ ■
Introduction: Experiments with Two or More Independent Variables

In the experiments discussed in the last three chapters, we have manipulated only one independent variable. Sometimes it is necessary to manipulate more than one independent variable in order to fully understand what causes a behavior. The general term for any design with more than one independent variable is **factorial design**.

Langer, Blank, and Chanowitz (1978) conducted an experiment using a factorial design. The goal of the study was to see if people would mindlessly comply with requests. They approached people at the copy machine and asked to cut in line using one of three requests:

1. Excuse me, I have five (twenty) pages. May I use the Xerox machine?
2. Excuse me, I have five (twenty) pages. May I use the Xerox machine because I have to make copies?
3. Excuse me, I have five (twenty) pages. May I use the Xerox machine because I'm in a rush?

The first request provided no reason for cutting in line. The second request provided a reason, but this reason was not valid as an excuse to cut (it is obvious that a person wanting to use the Xerox machine would like to make copies). The

METHODOLOGY NOTE 7.1   Even though there are two independent variables in the Langer, Blank, and Chanowitz (1978) study, the same metaphor applies as in one-way designs. Think of independent variables as the names of dimensions, with levels lined up along each dimension. One independent variable in Langer et al.'s experiment is request type, and it has three levels: no reason, empty reason, and valid reason. The other independent variable is size of request, and it has two levels, five pages and twenty pages. The request type dimension is the amount of reason in the request, from none to valid. The size of request dimension is number of copies. In each case, Langer et al. picked levels at various points along the dimension to cover the range.

third request had a valid reason to cut (being in a rush). If people mindlessly comply, then any reason should be sufficient to be allowed to cut in line. If people do not mindlessly comply, then only a valid reason should get compliance with the request. Langer et al. also used two amounts when they made their requests (five copies or twenty copies). They wanted to find out if the size of the request affected compliance.

Crossing three levels of request with two sizes of requests produces a 3 × 2 factorial design. The first number in the name refers to the number of levels of the first independent variable. The second number is the number of levels of the second independent variable. The multiplication sign is read "by." There is a lot of information in this notation. With Langer et al.'s (1978) design (3 × 2) you would know:

1. *That there were two independent variables.* Each number represents one independent variable.
2. *That there were three levels of the first variable and two levels of the second.* Each number is a number of levels.
3. *That there are six conditions are in the experiment.* Treat the name as a multiplication problem, and you get six conditions in the experiment.

How do you know what will happen in each condition? The best way is to make a chart, as in Figure 7.1.

A person in condition 1 will be given no reason for making five copies. A person in condition 6 will be given a valid reason for making twenty copies. For two-group experiments, we flipped a coin to randomly assign people to conditions. For a complex design like this, we would have to use a random number table. Start at a random location in the random number table and write down the first six numbers between one and six in the order you encounter them. Then, assign your first six participants to conditions using these numbers. For example, in my random number table, 3 is the first number I encountered. So, my first participant would get a valid reason for five copies. Repeat in multiples of six until everyone has been run.

Figure 7.1   The design of the Langer, Blank, and Chanowitz (1978) experiment.

Request Type

	No Reason	Empty Reason	Valid Reason
5	None 5 (1)	Empty 5 (2)	Valid 5 (3)
20	None 20 (4)	Empty 20 (5)	Valid 20 (6)

Size of Request

As in one-way designs, you can run a factorial design between participants or within participants. For between-participants designs, every person would be in one and only one condition. For within-participants designs, every person would be in every condition. With factorial designs, you have another option in addition to between and within participants; you can run a **mixed design**. In a mixed design, you have at least one between-participants variable and at least one within-participants variable. This allows you to take advantage of some of the benefits of within-participants designs even if you cannot run all of the independent variables within participants.

We have already considered one reason to use factorial designs. Basically, in the real world, multiple variables operate to produce a behavior. If you do not include them all in your design, you are not going to understand the full relationship. For Langer et al. (1978) the concern is that the size of the request may combine with the type of request to affect compliance. There are two other good reasons to do factorial designs: efficiency and information.

1. *Efficiency.* By combining multiple simple experiments into one large experiment, you can gather more information in less time. This is especially true if you use a within-participants or mixed design.

2. *Information.* There are two sorts of information available after you conduct a factorial design. The first sort of information is about **main effects**. These are the effects of a single variable. Looking at a main effect is similar to looking at the results of a one-way design with just that variable in it. The question you can address is: What effect does this variable have all by itself? You will have one main effect for each independent variable in your design.

Langer et al. (1978) had two main effects, request type and size of request. What were the results for the two main effects? For request type, people were less likely to comply when no reason was given ($M = 42\%$) than when a reason was given. When a reason was given, participants were less likely to comply with the empty reason ($M = 58\%$) than with the valid reason ($M = 68\%$). This main effect was significant. As you might have expected, for the size of the

Figure 7.2 Graph of the type of request × size of favor interaction from Table 1 of Langer, Blank, and Chanowitz (1978).
Source: From "The mindlessness of ostensibly thoughtful action: The role of 'placebic' information in interpersonal interaction," by E. Langer, A. Blank, and B. Chanowitz, 1978, *Journal of Personality and Social Psychology, 36,* pp. 635–642. Copyright © 1978 by the American Psychological Association. Used with permission.

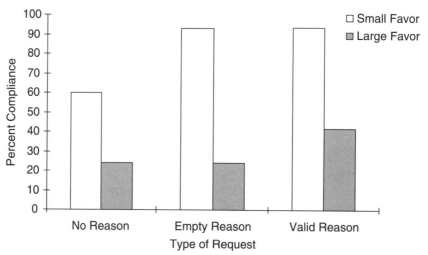

request people were more likely to comply when the request was small (*M* = 82%) than when the request was large (*M* = 30%). This main effect was also significant.

The real gain from doing factorial research is to look at interactions. An **interaction** is the combined effect of two or more variables. Interpreting an interaction can be tricky. Let's look at the interaction from Langer et al.'s (1978) experiment. A graph of their interaction is presented in Figure 7.2.

First, the technical definition of an interaction is "the effect of one variable is different at different levels of the other variable." So, what we are looking to see is if the effect of request type is different for the two favor sizes. Langer et al. (1978) predicted that there would be an interaction. They expected mindless compliance when the favor was small and a reason was given in the request (either "I have to make copies" or "I'm in a rush"). When the favor was large, they expected compliance only when a valid reason was given ("I'm in a rush").

As you can see, for a small favor, people comply just as much with an empty reason as with a valid reason. For a large favor, the rate of compliance for an empty reason is as low as for no reason. In other words, mindless compliance only seems to apply to small favors and not large ones. Note how we could not make that conclusion if we had not measured two types of favor. If we had had only small favors, we would have made the erroneous conclusion that people mindlessly comply with requests. If we had had only a large favor, we would have made the erroneous conclusion that people do not mindlessly comply.

The results of an interaction between a person's mood and the environment will be important for our target article for this chapter. Basically, we will test the theory that a person's mood will influence his or her perception of the world. The interaction will arise because information consistent with mood should be perceived more easily than information that is inconsistent. In other words, happy people should perceive happy information more easily than sad information, and sad people should perceive sad information more easily than happy information.

■ ■ ■ ■ ■ ■
Target Article: Mood and Perception

Our target article for this chapter was written by Niedenthal and Setterlund (1994). The basic issue is this: Will a person's mood affect how he or she perceives the world? For example, will sadness lead a person to perceive sad events more readily than happy events? The answer to these questions can have interesting theoretical implications. For example, we might be able to understand the role that emotions play in perception and memory. On a more practical level, we might gain insight about potential therapeutic interventions.

Experimental evidence about the relationship between mood and perception has been mixed. Gerrig and Bower (1982) hypnotized participants and then placed them in either an angry mood or a happy mood by having them recall a specific event from their lives that made them angry or happy at the time it happened. Participants then saw words for a very brief duration. Some of these words matched their mood (e.g., *pain* for angry) and some mismatched (e.g., *glee* for angry). After the word disappeared, participants saw a pair of words (the original word and a word that differed from it by one letter) and chose the one that had previously been presented. The idea was that people

---

METHODOLOGY NOTE 7.2   Gerrig and Bower (1982) had a potential problem with **demand characteristics**. A demand characteristic is some aspect of the experiment that allows participants to guess the hypothesis. Once participants know the hypothesis, they can attempt to produce data consistent with it. This can make conclusions difficult to draw. In Gerrig and Bower's case, the problem had to do with the mood manipulation. Participants may have noticed that some words matched the mood that was suggested to them, and they may have tried harder on those words. If Gerrig and Bower had found a difference, it might have been due to demand characteristics. When you design your study, it helps to think like a participant and look for clues that might suggest the hypothesis. If possible, remove those clues from the design.

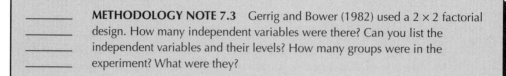

_____ **METHODOLOGY NOTE 7.3** Gerrig and Bower (1982) used a 2×2 factorial
_____ design. How many independent variables were there? Can you list the
_____ independent variables and their levels? How many groups were in the
_____ experiment? What were they?

would have an easier time perceiving the word that matched their mood, which
would make it easier to choose the correct word from the pair and cause them
to respond more accurately. This did not happen. People were just as accurate
for mood-incongruent words as for mood-congruent words.

Small (1985) criticized some aspects of the Gerrig and Bower (1982) experiments. The basic complaint was with the words that were used. Small selected new words that provided a better fit between the mood and the words
(as determined by independent raters). To induce the mood, Small used the
Velten (1968) mood induction task. He induced two moods, depressed and
neutral. To induce a mood, he asked people to read statements off cards and
to imagine those statements applying to themselves. Depressed statements included "I feel rather sluggish now." Neutral statements were things such as
"99.1% of Alaska is owned by the federal government."

After the mood was induced, Small (1985) presented words on a tachisto-
scope (a device that allows visual presentation for very short durations). The
goal was to see how long a word had to be presented before it could be recognized. Small presented depression words and neutral words. Small started with
100 ms (1/10 of a second). If the word was not recognized, he added 10 ms
and showed it again. This was repeated until the person could recognize the
word. The idea was that people would need less time to recognize a mood-
congruent word. This is what happened. Depressed participants recognized
depression words 13 ms faster than neutral words. Neutral participants recognized both kinds of word at about the same speed.

Our target article suggests a reason that the results from mood and perception experiments sometimes show a difference based on mood (as in Small,
1985) and sometimes do not (as in Gerrig and Bower, 1982). Niedenthal and
Setterlund (1994) hypothesized that only the perception of information that
specifically matches the mood will be affected. Perception of information that
has the same valence as the mood but does not match it will not necessarily be
affected by mood. So, if a person is in a sad mood, sad information will be

_____ **METHODOLOGY NOTE 7.4** Small (1985) used a 2×2 factorial design. Can
_____ you list the independent variables and their levels? How many groups were in
_____ the experiment? What were they?

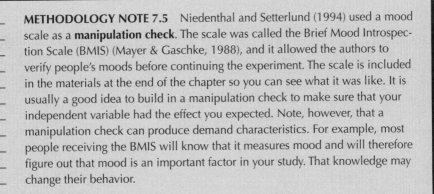

METHODOLOGY NOTE 7.5 Niedenthal and Setterlund (1994) used a mood scale as a **manipulation check**. The scale was called the Brief Mood Introspection Scale (BMIS) (Mayer & Gaschke, 1988), and it allowed the authors to verify people's moods before continuing the experiment. The scale is included in the materials at the end of the chapter so you can see what it was like. It is usually a good idea to build in a manipulation check to make sure that your independent variable had the effect you expected. Note, however, that a manipulation check can produce demand characteristics. For example, most people receiving the BMIS will know that it measures mood and will therefore figure out that mood is an important factor in your study. That knowledge may change their behavior.

more easily perceived. Negative information that is not necessarily sad (such as anger words) will not receive a perceptual advantage. Alternatively, if a person is happy, happy information will be perceived more easily. Generally positive information (like calming words) will not be affected.

To test this, Niedenthal and Setterlund (1994) had to create word lists that were happy (*delight*), generally positive (*calm*), sad (*weep*), generally negative (*injury*), and neutral (*habit*). They induced people to happy or sad moods by playing either happy music or sad music. Participants completed a scale to allow the authors to determine if the correct mood had been induced.

To measure perception, participants saw a list of letter strings and verified whether or not the strings were real words. This type of task is called "lexical decision." A person who saw *nexat* would say "not a word"; and one who saw *humor* would say "word." The trick was that some words specifically matched the mood; some were in the direction of the mood but were not specific matches; and some were neutral. The hypothesis was that lexical decisions would be fastest only for words that specifically matched a person's mood.

METHODOLOGY NOTE 7.6 Niedenthal and Setterlund (1994) used a 2 × 5 factorial design. The first independent variable was mood, and it had two levels: happy and sad. The second independent variable was word type, and it had five levels: happy, positive, neutral, negative, and sad. There were ten groups in the experiment. Niedenthal and Setterlund used a mixed design to take partial advantage of the benefits of a within-participants design. They manipulated mood between participants, but word type was manipulated within participants. Why do you think mood was not also manipulated within participants?

Figure 7.3 Graph of the word type × mood interaction from Table 3 of Niedenthal and Setterlund (1994).

Source: From "Emotion congruence in perception," by P. M. Niedenthal and M. B. Setterlund, 1994, *Personality and Social Psychology Bulletin, 20,* pp. 401–411. Copyright © 1994 Sage Publications, Inc. Used with permission.

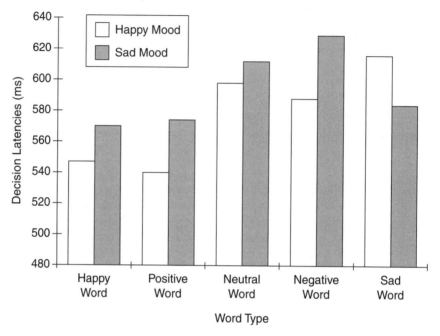

The interesting result was the word type × mood interaction. This interaction was significant and is presented graphically in Figure 7.3.

Direct your attention to the data from the happy words and the sad words. Note that happy participants were faster for happy words than sad participants. On the other hand, sad participants were faster for sad words than happy participants. This interaction was not present for the words that were generally positive or generally negative. This is consistent with Niedenthal and Setterlund's 1994 hypothesis that there would only be an effect on perception if the mood and word specifically matched.

You may have noticed that the difference in perception amounts to around 28 ms (.028 seconds). This is a very small amount of time in the real world (even though it is statistically significant). Small's 1985 effect was 13 ms (.013 second). Could effects of this magnitude have any impact on people's behavior, or are they just something that occurs in these relatively constrained laboratory conditions? That is an important question, and some of the suggested projects below will allow you to explore the issue for yourself.

■ ■ ■ ■ ■ ■
Implementing the Design

Materials

The first section of the materials contains suggestions for manipulating mood. Some of these techniques will require you to gather materials from other sources. Complete instructions and statements for the Velten mood induction procedure (used by Small, 1985, above) have been included.

The second section of the materials describes the BMIS test that Niedenthal and Setterlund (1994) used as a manipulation check. Other tests of mood are also described.

The third section of the materials describes *Lexical Decision Task* software that will allow you to replicate Niedenthal and Setterlund's (1994) experiment.

If you do not have access to a computer, this experiment could also be implemented in a paper-and-pencil format. Randomly order each kind of word with an equal number of nonwords. For example, arrange six sad words with six nonwords. Print each kind of word on a separate sheet and time people as they make decisions to all of the words on the sheet (for example, you might time a sad sheet and a happy sheet). Record errors on a score sheet as participants make the decisions.

This will not be as accurate as computerized presentation, but you can get reasonably close. This method may be more likely to suggest the hypothesis to participants, so you should ask them to guess the hypothesis at the end. Anyone who figured out the design of the experiment could be removed from the analysis.

■ Manipulating Mood

❏ *The Velten Mood Induction Procedure*
The procedure was originally developed by Emmett Velten in his doctoral dissertation (Velten, 1967). Validation data for the technique were presented in

> **ETHICS NOTE 7.1**   Manipulating mood raises an ethical issue. It is possible that manipulating a person into a negative or depressed mood may cause harm (particularly if the participant is already susceptible to such moods). Most of the techniques described below only create mild moods, and these moods generally last only a short time. However, you should research your mood manipulations carefully to be sure that the potential for harm is minimized as much as possible. On your informed consent sheet, you should list any potential risks that you uncover. There may be some people who should be discouraged from participating.

Velten (1968). The statements Velten used in his dissertation are reproduced in the first chapter supplement. If you plan to use this task, some of the statements may need to be modified or deleted. One statement refers to the war in Vietnam. Several statements refer to college students, which would not be relevant for a noncollege population.

The procedure for administering the Velten task was as follows (taken from Velten, 1967). Participants read statements off index cards. The participants read each statement twice, once to themselves, once out loud. They were instructed to think of each statement over and over again with the determination to really believe it. Participants were to use whatever technique worked for them to feel whatever mood was being presented on each card. Two strategies were suggested: repeating the thoughts over and over, trying to believe them; and imagining scenes. Participants were instructed to give full attention to feeling the moods on the cards. They were told that the purpose was to see if a person could talk him- or herself into a mood. They were cautioned not to laugh, even though at some point they would probably feel like laughing. For the neutral mood, people were simply instructed to concentrate on the statements. Velten had participants read the instructions off cards to get them used to the task.

For the neutral condition, participants were told to read each statement silently, then out loud. They were to focus on each statement for the full time the card was in front of them.

❑ Musical Mood Induction

Niedenthal and Setterlund (1994) used a musical mood induction technique. For happy music, they played 12.5 minutes of allegros from Mozart's *Eine Kleine Nachtmusik, Divertimento No. 136*, Mozart's *Ein Musikalischer Spass*, excerpts from Vivaldi's *Concerto in C Major*, and Vivaldi's *Concerto in G Major*. For sad music, they played 15.5 minutes of selections from Barber's *Adagio for Strings*, Mahler's *Adagietto*, and Rachmaninov's adagio from *Piano Concerto No. 2 in C Minor*. The musical selections and procedure were based on Eich and Metcalfe (1989). The music was played for the amount of time Eich and Metcalfe found that it took for the mood to be induced.

Martin and Metha (1997) used a musical mood induction task to stimulate the recall of childhood memories. They found (among other things) that happy music tends to elicit more happy memories than sad music. I mention their study here because they also included a neutral musical mood induction condition. This is something that was missing from Niedenthal and Setterlund (1994).

❑ Using Gifts to Induce Positive Mood

Isen, Shalker, Clark, and Karp (1978) hypothesized that people in a positive mood would make more positive judgments than people in a negative mood. Participants were drawn from people in a local mall. To manipulate mood, they gave a gift to half of the participants (retail value 29 cents) and no gift to the other half. Then, participants were presented with (what they thought was) an unrelated product survey about their automobile and television set. People who had received the gift rated their products more highly than people who received no gift.

❏ *Other Mood Induction Techniques*

Other techniques are also used to induce mood. Blaney (1986) includes a nice table outlining the type of mood manipulation used by various researchers, what their research questions were, and what they found. This type of review may be a good place to start if you are interested in exploring other sorts of mood induction.

Westermann, Spies, Stahl, and Hesse (1996) present a meta-analysis of 250 effect sizes (from an original sample of 138 studies). They compare the effectiveness of the various mood induction procedures and recommend the film/story technique (with explicit mood instructions) as the best way to induce positive mood. Film/story and most of the other techniques they considered were equally effective at inducing negative mood.

■ Mood Manipulation Checks

❏ *The BMIS*

Niedenthal and Setterlund (1994) used the BMIS to assess whether or not participants were in the correct mood. That scale is reproduced in the second chapter supplement, along with scoring instructions.

❏ *Other Manipulation Checks*

These are all taken from Velten's (1967) dissertation:

1. *Writing speed*. Velten (1967) cites an unpublished paper by Velten and DeNike (1966) that used writing speed as a manipulation check. Participants were instructed to write down numbers in descending order, starting at 100. No mention was made of the fact that the test was being timed. Depressed participants should write fewer numbers.
2. *Distance estimation*. Velten (1967) cites an experiment by Johnson (1937) showing that elated people make larger distance estimations than depressed people. A yardstick was placed along the edge of a table. Participants were to estimate 12, 18, and 24 inches by spreading their hands. They then moved their hands down to the yardstick, and the accuracy of the estimate was recorded.
3. *Decision time*. Johnson (1937) also found that decision time is slower for depressed people. Velten (1967) gave people five pairs of weights and asked them to decide which was heavier. The time to make these decisions was recorded.
4. *Word association*. Velten (1967) cites a study by Fisher and Marrow (1934) that found that depressed people are slower to make word associations.

Velten had people say the first thing that came to mind for the following list of words: *paper, wood, show, snow, birds, life, music, happy, sex, love, parent, sorrow, fear, accident, hate,* and *school*. Velten recorded the time to make an association to each word.

■ **The *Lexical Decision Task* Software**

The software will allow you to present the experiment described by Niedenthal and Setterlund (1994). You can use the default settings of the software to recreate Niedenthal and Setterlund's experiment, or you can create your own word lists and modify the software to present them. Follow the installation instructions in Appendix E to install the software from the CD.

❏ *Setting Up the Word Lists*

Using the default word list   The word list that comes with the program contains the words from Niedenthal and Setterlund (1994). The nonwords were created to be as similar to their nonwords as possible. The parameter set in the "Experiments" folder will automatically link to this list.

Creating your own word list   Before you create your own word list, you should print the word list that comes with the software. You should also look over the word list template. The rules for creating a word list are:

1. The first line of the file should be "LD Word File."
2. Each set of words should have a label (e.g., "positive_words"). The label will be on its own line before each set of words.
3. The words should be typed one per line below their label. Each condition must have the same number of words.
4. After all sets of words have been typed, type the nonwords. There must be as many nonwords as words, blocked into conditions. Each set of nonwords should also have a label ("nonwords_1," "nonwords_2," etc.).
5. After the nonwords, type the practice words (if any). The label "practice_words" should be typed before the practice words.
6. Finally, type the practice nonwords (with the label "practice_nonwords").
7. Spellcheck the words and then save the file as "text" so that the program can access it. For Windows users, the file extension must be ".txt." For Macintosh users, saving as "Text Only" will work.

Once you have your word list prepared, you are ready to run the program. There are two modes in which you can run the program.

❏ *Running an Experiment That Is Already Set Up*

To run Niedenthal and Setterlund's (1994) experiment, open the "Experiments" folder and double-click "LDT Experiment." If you run the standard experiment, the program will automatically load the correct parameters. All you need to do is enter a participant number and press "Enter." If you have already programmed your own experiment, double-clicking its parameter file will produce the same effect.

Figure 7.4 *Lexical Decision Task* word list parameters screen.

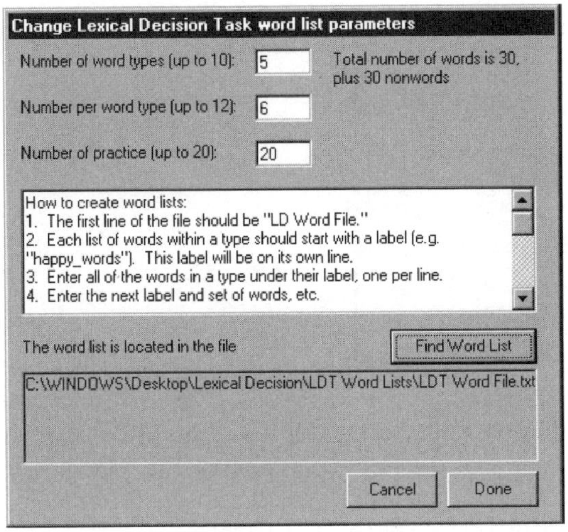

Change Lexical Decision Task word list parameters

Number of word types (up to 10): [5]   Total number of words is 30, plus 30 nonwords

Number per word type (up to 12): [6]

Number of practice (up to 20): [20]

How to create word lists:
1. The first line of the file should be "LD Word File."
2. Each list of words within a type should start with a label (e.g. "happy_words"). This label will be on its own line.
3. Enter all of the words in a type under their label, one per line.
4. Enter the next label and set of words, etc.

The word list is located in the file   [Find Word List]

C:\WINDOWS\Desktop\Lexical Decision\LDT Word Lists\LDT Word File.txt

[Cancel]   [Done]

❑ *Setting Up an Experiment*

To program your own experiment, double-click the *Lexical Decision Task* program. When the experiment is running, click the "Set Up" button. This will take you to the program's parameter screen.

There are two types of parameters that you will need to set before running an experiment. Word list parameters tell the program how many words to present and where they are located. Presentation parameters tell the program how to implement the experiment. Each will be discussed in turn.

Setting the word list parameters   Click the "Change" button by "Word List Parameters." You will get the screen in Figure 7.4.

You may have up to ten word types and twelve words per type. Niedenthal and Setterlund (1994) had five word types (happy, positive, sad, negative, and neutral), with six words per type. Enter the number of word types and the number per type for your experiment. Also, enter the number of practice trials (up to twenty). This is the number of words for practice plus the number of nonwords for practice. Set a path to the word list by clicking on the "Find Word List" button.

Click "Done" to return to the parameters screen.

Setting the presentation parameters   Click the "Change" button by "Presentation Parameters." You will get the screen in Figure 7.5.

The structure of a trial is:

fixation point
↓
blank interval
↓
letter string

Figure 7.5 *Lexical Decision Task* presentation parameters screen.

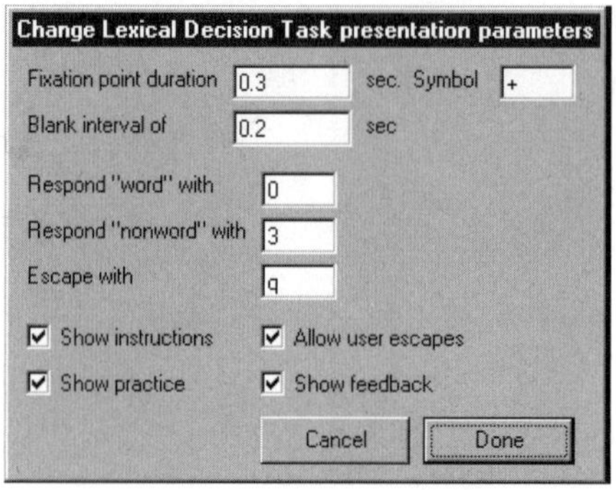

You may set the duration for the fixation point and the blank interval. You may also choose a character to use as a fixation point. Macintosh users may also set a response duration. The response duration is the maximum amount of time a person can wait before responding.

You can also set which keys will be used to respond "word" and "nonword" and which key will be used to escape the program early (if you choose to allow escapes).

If you check "Show instructions," the standard instructions will be presented. Check "Show practice" to present practice trials. Finally, you can decide whether or not you want feedback on the word judgments. If you check "Show feedback" the program will present "Correct!" or "Error!" after each response (for Macintosh users the program will beep when an error is made). Click "Done" when you finish setting presentation parameters.

On the main parameters screen, you will see a brief verbal description of all of your parameter settings. If everything looks OK, choose "Save Set-Up File." Name your parameter file and choose a location to save it. Whenever you want to run the experiment you have just set up, double-click your parameters file to launch the program. Click "Done" to return to the main screen. Enter a participant number and run the program to test your parameters. You should always test your parameter settings when you make a new experiment.

■ The *LDT Analysis* Software

When you finish collecting data, you will need to analyze it using the *LDT Analysis* software. You can view the results for a single participant or prepare a file with the results of an entire experiment. You will have to run the data files through the analysis program before you will be able to view the results.

❑ *Viewing a Participant's Data File*

To print a single participant's results, double-click that participant's data file. You will see the screen in Figure 7.6.

If you double-clicked a data file, you can click "Output," and the data will be processed. The file that is created will be saved in the same folder as the data

Figure 7.6 *LDT Analysis* output screen.

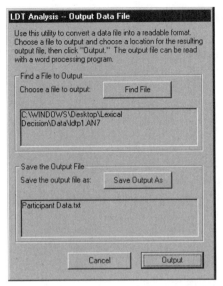

file and will be called "Participant Data." Double-clicking the file will allow you to see the results for that participant. If the analysis program is already running, chose "Output Data File" from the main window to get this screen. (Macintosh users will choose actions from the "Analysis Menu" in the menu bar.) Choose "Find File" to choose a file to print. Click "Save Output As" to create a file for the processed data. You will be asked to choose a name and location for the data file. Macintosh users have the option of sending a file to the printer, but this option may not always work correctly.

❑ *Analyzing a Group of Data Files*

If you double-click the *LDT Analysis* program and choose "Analyze Data" from the main screen, you will get the screen in Figure 7.7. (Macintosh users will choose actions from the "Analysis Menu" in the menu bar.)

For the analysis, you can choose to analyze reaction times or percent correct. If you choose reaction times, you can choose a central tendency to use to transform the reaction times in a condition to a single number. The transformations are median (the middle score), mean, or trimmed mean (the average after throwing out the top and bottom scores in a condition). You can also choose to include all reaction times or only those for which the response was correct.

The regular analysis will break your results into the various word types. You can also analyze only the nonwords by checking "Analyze Nonwords."

You will need to specify a path to the folder containing the data files. Simply open any data file, and the path will be set. The complete path for the data files will be displayed. You can specify a range of participant numbers to analyze. The program will only look for participant data files in the folder specified in the data file path.

Figure 7.7   *LDT Analysis* analysis screen.

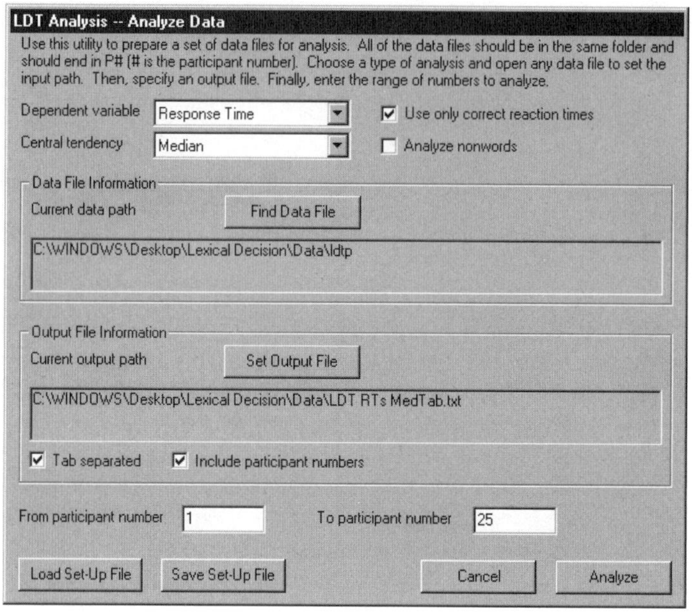

You can create a custom name for the output file, include participant numbers in the first column, and separate the output columns by spaces or tabs (choose whichever your statistics package prefers to import).

You can save and load your analysis parameters. Double-clicking an analysis parameter file will automatically reinstate your saved analysis, including data file paths.

Additional analysis help is available in the program. A demonstration of how to use the *Stroop Analysis* software is available in Appendix B. The *LDT Analysis* software will work the same way.

Suggested Projects

A word of caution: Be sure that none of the words used in your mood manipulation (for example the Velten cards) or your manipulation checks (like the BMIS) will appear on your word lists. If the same words are presented prior to the lexical decision task, you will probably find an effect, but it will likely be due to priming and not mood. You can avoid this potential confound by making sure the words used do not overlap, or you can build in a condition to explicitly show that any effects are due more to mood than priming. For example, you could use the words from the Velten cards without explicitly manipulating mood. If the amount of priming from this condition is less than any differences you find in your experimental conditions, you know that mood contributed something above and beyond priming.

☆ 1. You can replicate the original Niedenthal and Setterlund (1994) experiment. The musical selections that they used are listed in the materials above. The *Lexical Decision Task* software will allow you to present their experiment. You can use the BMIS as a manipulation check to assess mood.

   2. You can make minor modifications to the Niedenthal and Setterlund (1994) experiment. Some suggestions:

☆☆   a. Change the mood manipulation. Some of the techniques we have discussed so far are the Velten procedure (for which the materials have been provided), a music induction with different musical selections, giving gifts (only for positive mood), and watching a film with explicit mood instructions. Others (from Westermann et al., 1996) include an imagination condition (imagine situations from life that evoke the right mood), feedback (positive or negative information about performance on some task), and social interaction (interact with a person appearing to be in the desired mood).

      One really interesting technique (although the weakest according to Westermann et al., 1996) is to have a person configure his or her face into the expression the mood would produce. This can be achieved by instructing people to move individual muscles to make a smile or a frown. One version of this was used by Erber (1991). He had participants lightly grip a pen in their teeth (making a happy face) or tightly grip a pen in their teeth (making an angry face). He then looked at the effect of this mood induction on person perception (project 3a below).

☆☆   b. If you change the mood manipulation, you may want to consider some additional manipulation checks as well. The BMIS is somewhat transparent. What happens with a more indirect measure of mood?

   3. What other aspects of perception are affected by mood? Some suggestions of things to try:

☆☆   a. *Person perception.* Berkowitz and Troccoli (1990) investigated person perception. In their experiment, mood seemed to influence ratings of people (positive mood led to positive ratings and vice versa). Erber (1991) also investigated person perception. In one study, he induced mood with a story reading task. In a second study, he used a facial mood induction procedure (the pen procedure described above). After the mood induction, participants read about people who had positive and negative characteristics. They then estimated the likelihood that each person would behave in a manner that was consistent with either the positive or negative characteristics. The estimates of behavior matched a participant's mood. In other words, negative moods made people expect characters to act negatively, and positive moods made people expect characters to act positively. You could look at the effect of mood on person perception using some of the other mood induction procedures discussed above. Also, Niedenthal and Setterlund (1994) found that mood has to specifically match information in order to have an effect. How does this result relate to the results on person perception? What specific information are people responding to?

☆☆☆ b. *Face perception.* Halberstadt and Niedenthal (1997) used a musical mood induction procedure to induce sad, happy, and neutral moods. They then had participants rate the similarity of pairs of faces with happy and sad expressions (a morphing technique was used to get continuous variation from happy to sad). The hypothesis was that emotion information would be more relevant for people in an emotional state and would be more likely to guide their categorization of the faces. This was the case. Again, one might ask what specific information is being attended to? Another interesting question has to do with posture and body language. Besides faces, is there any other aspect of a person's appearance that would be more relevant for people in emotion states? One last thing here: Dion, Berscheid, and Walster (1972) found that "what is beautiful is good." People were rated more positively the more attractive they were. How might this effect interact with mood to produce a rating of a person (as in project 3a above) or a judgment about a person's face?

☆☆☆ c. You may be able to think of other things that should also be affected by mood. For example, some of my students investigated the effect of a musical mood induction on story continuations. They played some of the musical selections described above and had participants read the beginning of a neutral story. Participants then finished the story. They had an independent student rate each story continuation on a 10-point scale from very sad to very happy. They expected the continuations to match participants' moods.

■ ■ ■ ■ ■ ■
References

Berkowitz, L., & Troccoli, B. T. (1990). Feelings, direction of attention, and expressed evaluations of others. *Cognition and Emotion, 4,* 305–325.

Blaney, P. H. (1986). Affect and memory: A review. *Psychological Bulletin, 99,* 229–246.

Dion, K., Berscheid, E., & Walster, E. (1972). What is beautiful is good. *Journal of Personality and Social Psychology, 24,* 285–290.

Eich, E., & Metcalfe, J. (1989). Mood dependent memory for internal versus external events. *Journal of Experimental Psychology: Learning, Memory, and Cognition, 15,* 443–455.

Erber, R. (1991). Affective and semantic priming effects on category accessibility and interference. *Journal of Experimental Social Psychology, 27,* 480–498.

Fisher, V. E., & Marrow, J. (1934). Experimental study of moods. *Character and Personality, 2,* 201–208.

Gerrig, R. J., & Bower, G. H. (1982). Emotional influences on word recognition. *Bulletin of the Psychonomic Society, 19,* 197–200.

Halberstadt, J. B., & Niedenthal, P. M. (1997). Emotional state and the use of stimulus dimensions in judgment. *Journal of Personality and Social Psychology, 72,* 1017–1033.

Isen, A. M., Shalker, T. E., Clark, M., & Karp, L. (1978). Affect, accessibility of material in memory, and behavior: A cognitive loop? *Journal of Personality and Social Psychology, 36,* 1–12.

Johnson, W. B. (1937). Euphoric and depressed moods in normal subjects. *Character and Personality, 6,* 79–98.

Langer, E., Blank, A., & Chanowitz, B. (1978). The mindlessness of ostensibly thoughtful action: The role of "placebic" information in interpersonal interaction. *Journal of Personality and Social Psychology, 36,* 635–642.

Martin, M. A., & Metha, A. (1997). Recall of early childhood memories through musical mood induction. *The Arts in Psychotherapy, 24,* 447–454.

Mayer, J. D., & Gaschke, Y. N. (1988). The experience and meta-experience of mood. *Journal of Personality and Social Psychology, 55,* 102–111.

Niedenthal, P. M., & Setterlund, M. B. (1994). Emotion congruence in perception. *Personality and Social Psychology Bulletin, 20,* 401–411. Used with permission of the author.

Small, S. A. (1985). The effect of mood on word recognition. *Bulletin of the Psychonomic Society, 23,* 453–455.

Velten, E. C. (1967). *The induction of elation and depression through the reading of structured sets of mood-statements.* Unpublished doctoral dissertation, University of Southern California.

Velten, E. C. (1968). A laboratory task for induction of mood states. *Behaviour Research and Therapy, 6,* 473–482.

Velten, E., & DeNike, L. D. (1966). *Mood induction through experimentally controlled autosuggestion.* Unpublished manuscript.

Westermann, R., Spies, K., Stahl, G., & Hesse, F. W. (1996). Relative effectiveness and validity of mood induction procedures: A meta-analysis. *European Journal of Social Psychology, 26,* 557–580.

Velten Mood Induction Statements

Source: All statements are taken from "The induction of elation and depression through the reading of structured sets of mood-statements," by E. C. Velten, 1967, unpublished doctoral dissertation, University of Southern California. Used by permission.

ELATION STATEMENTS

You will need to cut these out and paste them on cards before using them.

1 Today is neither better nor worse than any other day.	**2** I *do* feel pretty good today, though.
3 I feel lighthearted.	**4** This might turn out to have been one of my good days.
5 If your attitude is good, then things are good, and my attitude is good.	**6** I've certainly got energy and self-confidence to spare.
7 I feel cheerful and lively.	**8** On the whole, I have very little difficulty in thinking.
9 My parents are pretty proud of me most of the time.	**10** I'm glad I'm in college—it's the key to success nowadays.

You will need to cut these out and paste them on cards before using them.

11 For the rest of the day, I bet things will go really well.	**12** I'm pleased that most people are so friendly to me.
13 My judgment about most things is sound.	**14** It's encouraging that as I get farther into my major, it's going to take less study to get good grades.
15 I'm full of energy and ambition—I feel like I could go a long time without sleep.	**16** This is one of those days when I can grind out schoolwork with practically no effort at all.
17 My judgment is keen and precise today. Just let someone try to put something over on me!	**18** When I want to, I can make friends extremely easily.
19 If I set my mind to it, I can make things turn out fine.	**20** I feel enthusiastic and confident now.

You will need to cut these out and paste them on cards before using them.

21 There should be opportunity for a lot of good times coming along.	**22** My favorite song keeps going through my head.
23 Some of my friends are so lively and optimistic.	**24** I feel talkative — I feel like talking to almost anybody.
25 I'm full of energy, and am really getting to like the things I'm doing on campus.	**26** I'm able to do things accurately and efficiently.
27 I know good and well that I can achieve the goals I set.	**28** Now that it occurs to me, most of the things that have depressed me wouldn't have if I'd just had the right attitude.
29 I have a sense of power and vigor.	**30** I feel so vivacious and efficient today—sitting on top of the world.

You will need to cut these out and paste them on cards before using them.

31	32
It would really take something to stop me now!	In the long run, it's obvious that things have gotten better and better during my life.

33	34
I know that in the future I won't overemphasize so-called "problems."	I'm optimistic that I can get along very well with most of the people I meet.

35	36
I'm too absorbed in things to have time for worry.	I'm feeling amazingly good today!

37	38
I am particularly inventive and resourceful in this mood.	I feel superb! I think I can work to the best of my ability.

39	40
Things look good— things look great!	I feel that many of my friendships will stick with me in the future.

You will need to cut these out and paste them on cards before using them.

41 I can find the good in almost anything.	**42** I feel so gay and playful today—I feel like surprising someone by telling a silly joke.
43 I feel an exhilarating animation in all I do.	**44** I feel highly perceptive and refreshed.
45 My memory is in rare form today.	**46** In a buoyant mood like this one, I can work fast and do it right the first time.
47 I can concentrate hard on anything I do.	**48** My thinking is clear and rapid.
49 Life is so much fun; it seems to offer so many sources of fulfillment.	**50** Things will be better and better today.

You will need to cut these out and paste them on cards before using them.

51 I can make decisions rapidly and correctly; and I can defend them against criticism easily.	**52** I feel industrious as heck—I want something to do!
53 Life is firmly in my control.	**54** I wish somebody would play some good loud music!
55 This is great—I really do feel good! I *am* elated about things.	**56** I'm really feeling sharp now.
57 This is just one of those days when I'm ready to go!	**58** I feel like bursting with laughter—I wish somebody would tell a joke and give me an excuse!
59 I'm full of energy.	**60** God, I feel great!

DEPRESSION STATEMENTS

You will need to cut these out and paste them on cards before using them.

1 Today is neither better nor worse than any other day.	**2** However, I feel a little low today.
3 I feel rather sluggish now.	**4** Sometimes I wonder whether school is all that worthwhile.
5 Every now and then I feel so tired and gloomy that I'd rather just sit than do anything.	**6** I can remember times when everybody but me seemed full of energy.
7 Too often I have found myself staring listlessly into the distance, my mind a blank, when I definitely should have been studying.	**8** It has occurred to me more than once that study is basically useless, because you forget almost everything you learn anyway.
9 People annoy me; I wish I could be by myself.	**10** I've had important decisions to make in the past, and I've sometimes made the wrong ones.

You will need to cut these out and paste them on cards before using them.

11 I *do* feel somewhat discouraged and drowsy—maybe I'll need a nap when I get home.	**12** Perhaps college takes more time, effort, and money than it's worth.
13 I'm afraid the war in Vietnam may get a lot worse.	**14** I just don't seem to be able to get going as fast as I used to.
15 There have been days when I felt weak and confused, and everything went miserably wrong.	**16** Just a little bit of effort tires me out.
17 I've had daydreams in which my mistakes have kept occurring to me—sometimes I wish I could start over again.	**18** I'm ashamed that I've caused my parents needless worry.
19 I feel terribly tired and indifferent to things today.	**20** Just to stand up would take a big effort.

You will need to cut these out and paste them on cards before using them.

21 I'm getting tired out—I can feel my body getting exhausted and heavy.	**22** I'm beginning to feel sleepy— my thoughts are drifting.
23 At times I've been so tired and discouraged that I went to sleep rather than face important problems.	**24** My life is tiresome—the same old thing day after day depresses me.
25 I couldn't remember things well right now if I had to.	**26** I just can't make up my mind; it's so hard to make simple decisions.
27 I want to go to sleep—I feel like just closing my eyes and going to sleep right here.	**28** I'm not very alert; I feel listless and vaguely sad.
29 I've doubted that I'm a worthwhile person.	**30** I feel worn out. My health may not be as good as it's supposed to be.

You will need to cut these out and paste them on cards before using them.

31 It often seems that no matter *how* hard I try, things still go wrong.	**32** I've noticed that no one seems to really understand or care when I complain or feel unhappy.
33 I'm uncertain about my future.	**34** I'm discouraged and unhappy about myself.
35 I've lain awake at night worrying so long that I hated myself.	**36** Things are worse now than when I was younger.
37 The way I feel now, the future looks boring and hopeless.	**38** My parents never really tried to understand me.
39 Some very important decisions are almost impossible for me to make.	**40** I feel tired and depressed; I don't feel like working on the things I know I must get done.

You will need to cut these out and paste them on cards before using them.

41 I feel horribly guilty about how I've treated my parents at times.	**42** I have the feeling that I just can't reach people.
43 Things are easier and better for other people than for me. I feel like there's no use in trying again.	**44** Often people make me very upset; I don't like to be around them.
45 It takes too much effort to convince people of anything; there's no point in trying.	**46** I fail in communicating with people about my problems.
47 It's so discouraging the way people don't really listen to me.	**48** I've felt so alone before that I could have cried.
49 Sometimes I've wished I could die.	**50** My thoughts are so slow and downcast. I don't want to think or talk.

You will need to cut these out and paste them on cards before using them.

51 I just don't care about anything; life just isn't any fun.	**52** Life seems too much for me anyhow—my efforts are wasted.
53 I'm so tired.	**54** I don't concentrate or move; I just want to forget about everything.
55 I have too many bad things in my life.	**56** Everything seems utterly futile and empty.
57 I feel dizzy and faint—I need to put my head down and not move.	**58** I don't want to do anything.
59 All of the unhappiness of my past life is taking possession of me.	**60** I want to go to sleep and never wake up.

NEUTRAL STATEMENTS

You will need to cut these out and paste them on cards before using them.

1 Oklahoma City is the largest city in the world in area, with 631.166 square miles.

2 Japan was elected to the United Nations almost 14 years after Pearl Harbor.

3 At the end appears a section entitled "Bibliography Notes."

4 We have two kinds of nouns denoting physical things: individual and mass nouns.

5 This book or any part thereof must not be reproduced in any form.

6 Agricultural products comprised seventy percent of the income.

7 Saturn is sometimes in conjunction, beyond the sun from Earth, and is not visible.

8 Some streets were still said to be listed under their old names.

9 The system is supervised by its board of regents.

10 There is a large rose-growing center near Tyler, Texas.

You will need to cut these out and paste them on cards before using them.

11 Many states supply milk for grammar school children.	**12** It is God's will that the fittest survive.
13 The typography, paper, and binding were of the highest quality.	**14** The machine dominated county posts for as long as anyone could remember.
15 The desk was old, and scratched into its surface were a profusion of dates, initials, and pleading messages.	**16** The Orient Express travels between Paris and Istanbul.
17 When the banyan bent down under its own weight, its branches began to take root.	**18** There isn't a scientific explanation for every UFO sighting.
19 The Hope Diamond was shipped from South Africa to London through the regular mail service.	**20** The review is concerned with the first three volumes.

You will need to cut these out and paste them on cards before using them.

21 The ship was ancient and would soon be retired from the fleet.	**22** Slang is a constantly changing part of the language.
23 There is a small article in the local newspaper which indicates acceptance of the kidnapper's terms.	**24** There are some forms in which no oath is required.
25 Intramatics finds mates for the lonely.	**26** 99.1% of Alaska is owned by the federal government.
27 Two men dressed as repairmen will appear shortly after the van pulls up.	**28** The wood was discolored as if it had been held in a fire.
29 A light was noticed in the dark outside, and it moved eerily toward the house.	**30** Painting in a few other non-European countries is treated in a separate volume.

You will need to cut these out and paste them on cards before using them.

31 A recent study revealed that one-half of all college students were unable to find summer jobs.	**32** Provoked arousal and orientation are accompanied by steeper negative shifts.
33 The names on the Christmas mailing list are alphabetically ordered.	**34** Significantly, these changes occur during the full moon.
35 West Samoa gained its independence in 1965.	**36** The magazine's report was slanted, as usual.
37 The map would prove useless as a beginning guide.	**38** The speaker outlined a plan whereby the current deficits could be eliminated.
39 Black-and-white pictures are arranged in ten sections.	**40** The voices come only at night and whisper words, terrible words.

You will need to cut these out and paste them on cards before using them.

41 The papers had been front-paging it for days.	**42** The notice made it clear that coffee breaks were being limited.
43 No man worked harder than he.	**44** Potter wrote numerous satires on social cynicism.
45 Boeing's main plant in Seattle employs 35,000 people.	**46** The doorkeeper was dressed in red.
47 During the next ten years, the group participated in politics.	**48** The organization depended on the people for support.
49 In 1965, Elizabeth made the first state visit by a British monarch to Germany in 56 years.	**50** It was their sixth consecutive best seller.

You will need to cut these out and paste them on cards before using them.

51 It all fitted in with the officer's story.	**52** The merger did not change the company's policy.
53 The mansion was rented by the delegation.	**54** Ninety occupations were listed as eligible for the grads in business.
55 Utah is the Beehive State.	**56** Changes were made in transport of lumber after the border incident.
57 The Chinese language has many dialects, including Cantonese, Mandarin, and Wu.	**58** Things were booming once again in the little gold rush town of Angel.
59 At low tide, the hulk of the old ship could be seen.	**60** A free sample will be given to each person who enters the store.

The Brief Mood Introspection Scale (BMIS)

Rate each item below using the following scale:

XX (definitely do not feel)	X (do not feel)	V (feel somewhat)	VV (definitely do feel)

1. Lively _____

2. Happy _____

3. Sad _____

4. Tired _____

5. Caring _____

6. Content _____

7. Gloomy _____

8. Jittery _____

9. Drowsy _____

10. Grouchy _____

11. Peppy _____

12. Nervous _____

13. Calm _____

14. Loving _____

15. Fed up _____

16. Active _____

For scoring:

1. Assign each item a rating of 1–4 (XX = 1, . . . , VV = 4).

2. Add up the total for the positive items (1, 2, 5, 6, 11, 13, 14, 16) and the negative items (3, 4, 7, 8, 9, 10, 12, 15).

3. Subtract the sad score from the happy score. The higher the score, the happier the person felt.

Source: Adapted from "The experience and meta-experience of mood," by J. D. Mayer and Y. N. Gaschke, 1988, *Journal of Personality and Social Psychology, 55,* pp. 102–111. Copyright © 1988 by the American Psychological Association. Adapted with permission.

Factorial Designs II

Does "he" have to be a man?

When you read the sentence *When a nurse is really tired, he may adminis-ter the wrong medicine*, are you surprised to encounter the pronoun *he*? Re-search has shown that when the gender of a pronoun mismatches the pre-sumed gender of an antecedent, it does slow reading. But *he* has historically been used as a gender-neutral pronoun. English seems to offer no clear alter-native for singular pronouns (although *he or she* is a popular choice). The au-thors of our target article for this chapter (Foertsch & Gernsbacher, 1997) demonstrate that there is an easily comprehended alternative. Their reading time experiments show that there are cases (like the sentence above) where the pronoun *they* can be used as a singular gender-neutral pronoun.

■ ■ ■ ■ ■ ■
Introduction: Experiments with Two or More Independent Variables

The target article for this chapter uses a factorial design. Factorial designs were discussed at length in the opening section of Chapter 7. If you have not already done so, you may want to read that before continuing here.

■ ■ ■ ■ ■ ■
Target Article: In Search of a Gender Neutral Pronoun

Historically, English speakers have had difficulty choosing a singular gender-neutral pronoun to use with nonreferential human antecedents. For example, if I want to say *When a veterinarian treats an animal, <pronoun> should consider the feelings of the animal's human companion as well*, what pro-noun should I use to complete the sentence? In the 19th century, an act of the British parliament declared that the appropriate pronoun would be *he* (Ng, 1990). That would leave us with the sentence *When a veterinarian treats an animal, he should consider . . .* In the last few decades, research has shown

> **METHODOLOGY NOTE 8.1**   A few terms might make the following discussion easier to follow. A pronoun is a type of **anaphor**. An anaphor refers back to something earlier in a text. The part of the text being referred to by a pronoun is the **antecedent**. The actual thing the pronoun refers to is the **referent**. So, in the sentence *Angela was so happy she hummed a little tune*, *she* is an anaphor that refers to the antecedent *Angela*. The actual person Angela is the referent of *she*. Sometimes, antecedents are nonreferential (they do not refer to any particular individual). For example, in the sentence *If a student has an exam, then he should study*, *he* is not referring to any particular student, so it has no referent.

that this choice of pronoun is inappropriate because *he* causes readers to assume that the person being referred to is male, even if that person could be female. Let's consider some of that research.

Gastil (1990) had participants read sentences such as *The average American believes he watches too much TV*. Participants then described any image that came to mind (such as a "fat guy sitting on a couch"). Gastil examined the content of these images to see if the person imagined was male or female. The independent variable was the pronoun used. The levels were *he*, *he/she*, or *they*. Men and women generated more male images for *he* than for *they* (*he/she* was mixed, with men interpreting it as male and women interpreting it as female). In other words, *he* produced more male imagery than female imagery, suggesting it is not interpreted generically.

MacKay and Fulkerson (1979) explicitly tested the extent to which a pronoun determines the gender of its antecedent. In their Experiment 1, participants read sentences such as *A lawyer must frequently argue his case out of court*. The gender of the antecedent was varied from stereotypically male (*lawyer*) to neutral (*student*) to stereotypically female (*secretary*). After each sentence, participants decided if the sentence could refer to one or more females. The results were that 87% of the judgments were in error (87% of the responses were "no, it cannot refer to one or more females"). There were high error rates for stereotypically male antecedents (90%), neutral antecedents (85%), and stereotypically female antecedents (88%). It appears that a masculine pronoun determines people's interpretation of the gender of the antecedent, even when the antecedent is neutral or stereotypically female. In other words, *he* is not treated by readers as generic; it is used to determine the gender of the antecedent.

He is not a generic pronoun. At this point, most people have been convinced of this fact, and careful writers avoid using *he* to refer to antecedents who could be either male or female. The problem is, what should be used instead? The APA publication manual (2001) suggests rephrasing, using plural nouns and pronouns, or dropping the pronoun entirely. They caution against using *he or she* or *she or he* "because the repetition can become tiresome" (p. 66). They also advise against using *he/she*, *(s)he*, and alternating between *he* and *she*. In other words, except for rephrasing the sentence, there is not a very good alternative. There is an alternative that the APA publication manual appears not to consider: Use *they* as a singular pronoun. For example, my sentence above would become *When a veterinarian treats an animal, they should consider . . .*

Can *they* be used this way? Or will *they* used as a singular pronoun disrupt comprehension? On one level, we can argue that *they* moving from strictly plural to plural and singular is merely following the precedent set by *you*. Can we find data to support the contention that *they* is an acceptable singular pronoun? That was the purpose of our target article for this chapter.

Experiment 1

Foertsch and Gernsbacher (1997) used a reading time task to determine if using *they* as a pronoun in sentences with singular antecedents causes problems for readers. There were four types of antecedents: stereotypically masculine, stereotypically feminine, neutral, and indefinite. Examples of each are:

1. A truck driver should never drive when sleepy, even if *he/she/they* may be struggling to make a delivery on time, because many accidents are caused by drivers who fall asleep at the wheel.
2. A nurse should have an understanding of how a medication works, even if *he/she/they* will not have any say in prescribing it, because nurses must anticipate how a patient will respond to the medication.
3. A runner should eat lots of pasta the night before a race, even if *he/she/they* would rather have a steak, because carbohydrates provide fuel for endurance events, while proteins do not.
4. Anybody who litters should be fined $50, even if *he/she/they* cannot see a trash can nearby, because littering is an irresponsible form of vandalism and should be punished.

Each sentence contained three clauses, and the sentences were presented one clause at a time. The middle clause was the critical one. It always started with the equivalent of "even if" and contained either *he*, *she*, or *they*. This pronoun could match, mismatch, or be neutral with respect to the stereotypical gender of the antecedent. Participants pressed a button to advance through the clauses and read at their own pace. The important predictions had to do with how fast the second (critical) clause was read.

What predictions can we make about reading time for the critical clauses? Let's focus on the stereotypically masculine and stereotypically feminine

METHODOLOGY NOTE 8.2   Foertsch and Gernsbacher (1997) are using a 4 (antecedent type: stereotypically masculine, stereotypically feminine, neutral, indefinite) × 3 (pronoun: *he, she, they*) factorial design for this experiment. The design is within participants, because each participant will read some of each kind of text. Can you list the groups in their design and describe what will happen to each group?

> **METHODOLOGY NOTE 8.3**   To be sure that participants were reading for comprehension, Foertsch and Gernsbacher (1997) had participants judge whether each sentence was true or false. Some form of comprehension question is usually included in reading time experiments to be sure that the results really reflect comprehension difficulty.

antecedents. If there is a mismatch between the gender of the pronoun and the stereotypical gender of the antecedent, reading should take longer than if there is a match. In the mismatch conditions, readers will realize that they have attributed the wrong gender to the antecedent, and some correction should be necessary to understand the sentence, slowing reading. How will *they* fit into this picture? All of the antecedents are singular. So, if *they* causes a problem when used with singular antecedents, *they* clauses should be read slowly (at least as slowly as mismatching clauses). If *they* does not cause problems when used with singular antecedents, then *they* clauses should be read as quickly as in the matching condition. The results from the stereotypically masculine and stereotypically feminine conditions for Foertsch and Gernsbacher's (1997) Experiment 1 are presented in Figure 8.1 (Figure 8.1 has been redrawn from their Figure 1; neutral and indefinite antecedents have been omitted).

Figure 8.1   The antecedent × pronoun interaction.
Source: Redrawn from "In search of gender neutrality: Is singular *they* a cognitively efficient substitute for generic *he*?" by J. Foertsch and M. A. Gernsbacher, 1997, *Psychological Science, 8,* 106–111, Fig. 1. Copyright © 1997 American Psychological Society. Used by permission of Blackwell Publishers and the author.

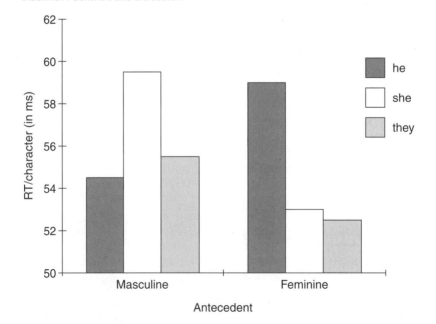

The dependent measure is reading time per character in ms (1/1000 of a second). To translate that to whole clause reading time, multiply by the average number of letters in the critical clauses (about 34 characters on average).

The results were clear. *They* clauses took no longer to read than gender-matched clauses. Gender-mismatched clauses did take longer. So, readers are not bothered by the plural pronoun *they* when it is used to refer to a singular antecedent. Note that *he* and *she* are both poor candidates for generic pronouns. Whenever the gender of the pronoun did not match the stereotypical gender of the antecedent, reading was slowed. This fits nicely with the APA *Publication Manual*'s (2001) claim that alternating between *he* and *she* is a bad idea because neither of them is gender neutral, and using them as if they were will confuse readers.

Experiment 2

None of the sentences in Experiment 1 referred to a particular person, just a class of people. This was indicated to readers by the indefinite determiner. For example, "A nurse should have . . ." suggests the general class of nurses, not any particular nurse. This makes the antecedent ("nurse") nonreferential. If the sentence was "*My* nurse should have. . ." it would suggest that the speaker has some particular nurse in mind. In the referential case, the speaker should know the gender of the nurse. Will it slow readers if *they* is used to refer to singular antecedents whose gender should be known to the speaker?

As in Experiment 1, we would expect clauses with matching pronouns to be read faster than mismatching clauses. It is harder to predict what will happen with *they* clauses. It certainly seems odd to say something like *When my dentist cleans my teeth, they always ask me questions when I cannot speak*. Will readers be slowed if *they* is used as an anaphor with a referential antecedent? The results were that *they* clauses were understood more slowly than matched clauses. Mismatched clauses took the longest to comprehend.

So, when the antecedent is referential (the speaker should know the gender), it seems odd to use *they* as the pronoun. When the antecedent is nonreferential (there is not really a gender for the antecedent because it is not referring to anyone in particular), *they* is fine for a singular pronoun.

■ ■ ■ ■ ■ ■
Implementing the Design

Materials

You have two options for replicating the Foertsch and Gernsbacher (1997) experiments.

If you do not have access to a computer, this experiment could be implemented in a paper-and-pencil format. One way would be to type each clause onto a separate notecard. You would have to type the critical clauses once with each pronoun. Have people read each clause out loud and time them for the critical clause with a precise stopwatch. This will not be as accurate as computerized presentation, but you can get pretty close.

Another suggestion would be to type several texts onto a sheet of paper and time people reading the whole sheet. For example, you might type one mismatching version with each type of antecedent on one sheet, one matching version on another sheet, and a neutral version on the third. The timing using this method would be a little crude, and it would be more likely to suggest the hypothesis to participants, so you would need to be careful in your design.

You may also use the software provided with this chapter to present the experiments in the projects section (this is the recommended technique). There are several steps involved. First, you have to either choose from the sample stimuli or create your own. Then, you have to set up your experiment using the software. Once the data are collected, you will have to use the analysis software to view the results.

■ The *Reading Time Experiment* Software

To implement your own experiments you will need the *Reading Time Experiment* software. This software allows you to replicate the original Foertsch and Gernsbacher (1997) experiments. You may also customize the software to present your own experiments. Follow the installation instructions in Appendix E to install the software from the CD.

❑ *Setting Up the Stimuli*

Using the sample stimuli   The stimuli for reading time experiments are text files. Three sets of text files have been included with the software.

1. *Foertsch and Gernsbacher (1997) Experiment 1.* There are 75 text files in the "FGE1 Texts" folder. Each file contains one text from the experiment. There is also a master text file that contains all of the texts. Use these texts to replicate Foertsch and Gernsbacher's Experiment 1.
2. *Foertsch and Gernsbacher (1997) Experiment 2.* There are 57 text files in the "FGE2 Texts" folder. Each file contains one text from the experiment. There is also a master text file that contains all of the texts. Use these texts to replicate Foertsch and Gernsbacher's Experiment 2.
3. *Langston, Ohnesorge, Keith, Scott, and Springer (1997).* There are 31 text files in the "LO Texts" folder. Each file contains one text from the experiment. There is also a master text file that contains all of the texts. Use these texts for project 2e.

Creating your own stimuli   You will need to create a custom text file before presenting your own texts. First, make a file with all of the texts in it. Use one of the sample files as a template. Some general guidelines:

1. The first line of each text is a dummy string that identifies it. For example, "FGE1Text." The program will ignore this string, but it will allow you to identify the experiment with which the text is associated.

2. Each line in the text file will be presented as a separate line in the experiment. So, if you are presenting sentences one clause at a time, enter each clause on a separate line (separate the lines by hitting "return"). If you are presenting texts one sentence at a time, enter each sentence on a separate line. All texts must have the same number of lines.

3. Windows users *must* enclose each line of the text file in quotation marks (" "). Failure to do so will result in text errors when the files are loaded for presentation. Do not use quotation marks within a line. Apostrophes (') are acceptable.

4. Sort the texts by condition. For example, have all stereotypically masculine antecedent texts in one batch, then all stereotypically feminine antecedent texts in another batch, and so on. You must have the same number of texts in each condition.

5. Wherever you want the program to insert a pronoun, put "@" in the text file. For example, "even if @ would rather have a steak" will cause the program to place a pronoun between "if" and "would." The program will randomly choose which pronoun to insert out of the set you specify.

6. Type any practice texts at the end of the file. You may have as many practice texts as you want to present. Include pronouns in the practice texts. The software will not insert pronouns into the practice texts.

7. You may ask a true/false or yes/no question after each text. After the text, type the question on its own line. If you want to score these questions, also type the answer on the line below the question. For "true" and "yes" responses, type "true" on the last line. For "false" and "no" responses, type "false" on the last line. The file "LO Text List" included in the "LO Texts" folder in the "Texts" folder has a sample file with questions.

8. Spell check the file and verify that the texts are correct.

Once the text file is created, save it as "Text Only." Use the *TextWriter* utility to break the master text file into files for individual texts. The screen for the *TextWriter* utility is presented in Figure 8.2.

Figure 8.2 *TextWriter* set-up screen.

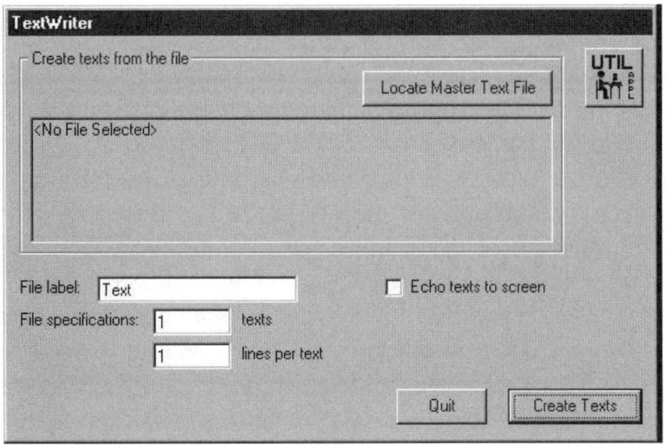

To use the *TextWriter* utility:

1. Click on "Locate Master Text File" and set a path to the text list you just created.
2. Enter a file label to name the texts. For example, for Foertsch and Gernsbacher's (1997) Experiment 1, the label was "FGE1Text"; the text number will be appended to this label (e.g., "FGE1Text1").
3. Enter the number of texts and number of lines per text. Count the dummy string as a line.
4. If you want to see what texts were processed after the files have been created, click "Echo texts to screen." This option is slower, but it is useful for error checking, especially the first time you build a set of text files.
5. When you finish, open some of the files to be sure the program operated correctly. If the files are not processed correctly, check your master text list and run the utility again.

❑ *Running an Experiment That Is Already Set Up*

To run Foertsch and Gernsbacher's (1997) Experiment 1 or 2, open the "Experiments" folder and double-click the experiment you want. If you run a standard experiment, the program will automatically load the correct parameters. All you need to do is enter a participant number and press "Begin." If you have already programmed your own experiment, double-clicking its parameter file will produce the same effect.

The settings for Langston et al. (1997) (project 2e below) are also in the "Experiments" folder and are called "LO Parameters." To run this experiment, double-click its parameter set.

❑ *Setting Up an Experiment*

To program your own experiment, double-click the *Reading Time Experiment* program. When the experiment is running, click the "Set Up" button. This will take you to the program's parameter screen.

There are two types of parameters that you will need to set before running an experiment. Stimulus parameters tell the program how many stimuli to present and where they are located. Presentation parameters tell the program how to implement the experiment. Each will be discussed in turn.

Setting the stimulus parameters   Click the "Change" button by "Stimulus Parameters." You will get the screen in Figure 8.3.

Enter the number of texts you will be presenting and the number of practice texts. Next, enter the number of lines per text and which line number you want timed. Finally, enter the number of conditions. The number of texts should be a multiple of the number of conditions, so that there will be the same number of texts in each condition. If your texts have questions, click the check box for "Text files include a question."

You may choose to use a standard set of pronouns from the pronoun pop-up menu, or you may choose "Custom" to enter your own set of pronouns.

Figure 8.3 *Reading Time Experiment* stimulus parameters screen.

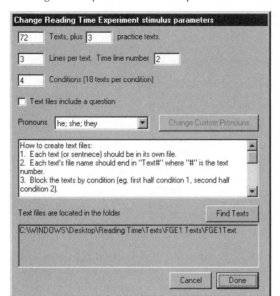

For custom pronouns, enter each pronoun on its own line; separate each line by hitting "return." The number of pronouns should divide evenly into the number of texts per condition.

Finally, set a path to the text files by clicking "Find Texts" and opening any individual text file for your experiment (do not use the master text file for this path). Any time you launch from these settings, the program will always follow this path to find the texts. If you move folders around after setting the path, you will need to do this step again. So, do not perform this step until you have all of the text folders where you want to leave them. As long as the folders are located in the same place on all machines, you can set up parameters on one machine and use the same paths on other machines. The best approach is to leave all text folders in the "Reading Time" folder.

Click "Done" to return to the parameters screen.

Setting the presentation parameters Click the "Change" button by "Presentation Parameters." You will get the screen in Figure 8.4.

There are three types of parameters that govern the presentation.

1. *Timing.* You can have a delay before each clause or sentence. You can also set a pause between each sentence or text. All of these times are in seconds for Windows users or ms (1/1000 of a second) for Macintosh users. Instead of pausing between texts, you can choose to alert the participant that a new sentence or text is about to begin.
2. *Response keys.* Three keys control the presentation. The "advance" key moves through clauses or sentences of the text. Its default is the space bar.

Figure 8.4   *Reading Time Experiment* presentation parameters screen.

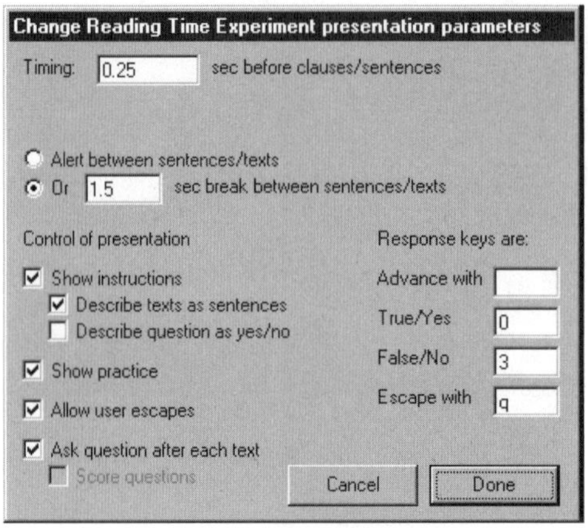

The "true/yes" key will be used to respond "true" or "yes." The "false/no" key will be used to respond "false" or "no." You can also set an "escape" key. This key can be typed by the participant to quit early.

3. *Control.* "Show instructions" will present standard instructions. Turn this off to present custom instructions. If you choose "Show instructions," "Describe texts as sentences" will describe clause-by-clause presentation; without this option, the instructions will describe sentence-by-sentence presentation. "Describe questions as yes/no" will present "yes/no" instructions. Without this option, the questions will be described as "true/false."

"Show practice" will present your practice texts. "Allow user escapes" will allow the participant to quit early with the escape key. "Ask question after each text" will present a question after each text. If you included questions in the text file, those will be presented. If there are no questions in the text file, "True or false?" will be presented. If you included questions in the text file, you may click "Score questions" to have the participants' answers checked. Click "Done" when you finish setting presentation parameters.

On the main parameters screen, you will see a brief verbal description of all of your parameter settings. If everything looks OK, choose "Save Set-Up File." Name your parameter file and choose a location to save it. Whenever you want to run the experiment you have just set up, double-click your parameters file to launch the program. Click "Done" to return to the main screen. Enter a participant number and run the program to test your parameters. You should always test your parameter settings when you make a new experiment.

■ The *RT Analysis* Software

When you finish collecting data, you will need to analyze it using the *RT Analysis* software. You can view the results for a single participant or prepare a file with the results of an entire experiment. You will have to run the data files through the analysis program before you will be able to view the results.

Figure 8.5 *RT Analysis* output screen.

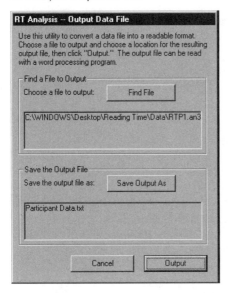

□ *Viewing a Participant's Data File*

To print a single participant's results, double-click that participant's data file. You will see the screen in Figure 8.5.

If you double-clicked a data file, you can click "Output" and the data will be processed. The file that is created will be saved in the same folder as the data file and will be called "Participant Data." Double-clicking the output file will allow you to see the results for that participant. If the analysis program is already running, chose "Output Data File" from the main window to get this screen. (Macintosh users will choose actions from the "Analysis Menu" in the menu bar.) Choose "Find File" to choose a file to print. Click "Save Output As" to create a file for the processed data. You will be asked to choose a name and location for the data file. Macintosh users have the option of sending a file to the printer, but this option may not always work correctly.

□ *Analyzing a Group of Data Files*

If you double-click the *RT Analysis* program and choose "Analyze Data" from the main screen, you will get the screen in Figure 8.6. (Macintosh users will choose actions from the "Analysis Menu" in the menu bar.)

This part of the analysis program will let you analyze the results of multiple data files. To run an analysis, first enter the number of conditions. This should be the same as the number of conditions used to present the experiment. Then enter the pronouns used. Again, these should be the same as those used for data collection.

You can choose to analyze response times or proportion correct (if the questions were scored). If you choose response times, you can choose to analyze the per-character reading times (used by Foertsch & Gernsbacher, 1997)

Figure 8.6 *RT Analysis* analysis screen.

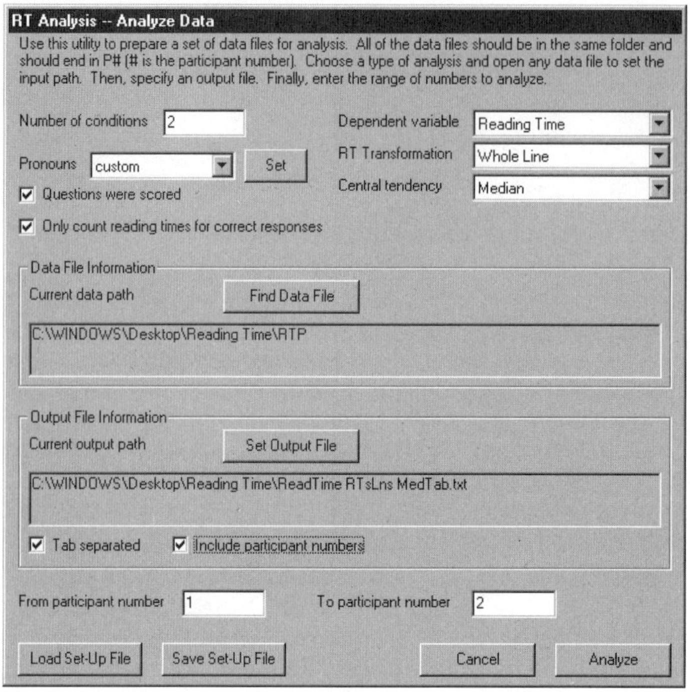

```
RT Analysis -- Analyze Data

Use this utility to prepare a set of data files for analysis. All of the data files should be in the same folder and
should end in P# (# is the participant number). Choose a type of analysis and open any data file to set the
input path. Then, specify an output file. Finally, enter the range of numbers to analyze.

Number of conditions    2              Dependent variable   Reading Time

Pronouns   custom    ▼     Set          RT Transformation    Whole Line

☑ Questions were scored                 Central tendency     Median

☑ Only count reading times for correct responses

Data File Information
Current data path        Find Data File

C:\WINDOWS\Desktop\Reading Time\RTP


Output File Information
Current output path      Set Output File

C:\WINDOWS\Desktop\Reading Time\ReadTime RTsLns MedTab.txt


☑ Tab separated    ☑ Include participant numbers


From participant number    1        To participant number    2

Load Set-Up File    Save Set-Up File          Cancel          Analyze
```

or whole clause (sentence) reading times. You can also choose the measure of
central tendency the program should use to transform the times in a condition
to a single number. The transformations are median (the middle score), mean,
or trimmed mean (the average after throwing out the top and bottom scores in
a condition). If you scored the questions, you can also choose to include all reaction times or only those for which the response was correct.

You will need to specify a path to the folder containing the data files. For
the program to work correctly, all data files need to be named "RTP#" where
the "#" is the participant number, and all data files need to be in the same
folder. The naming convention will automatically be followed if you use the default name from the main program. Simply open any data file, and the path
will be set. Windows users should also click "Set Output File" to set a path for
the output file (it will default to the data folder for Macintosh users). You can
create a custom name for the output file, include participant numbers in the
first column, and separate the output columns by spaces or tabs.

The complete paths for the data and output files will be displayed. You can
specify a range of participant numbers to analyze. The program will look for
participant data files only in the folder specified in the data file path.

You can save and load your analysis parameters. Double-clicking an analysis parameter file will automatically reinstate your saved analysis, including data
file paths.

Additional analysis help is available in the program. A demonstration of how to use the *Stroop Analysis* software is available in Appendix B. The *RT Analysis* software will work the same way.

Suggested Projects

☆ 1. You can replicate the Foertsch and Gernsbacher (1997) experiments. The "FGE1 Parameters" will allow you to replicate their Experiment 1. The "FGE2 Parameters" will allow you to replicate their Experiment 2.

   2. You can conduct experiments that are variations of the Foertsch and Gernsbacher (1997) experiments.

☆   a. Are there other possibilities for singular pronouns? Some researchers have looked at *he/she* (Gastil, 1990). You may also have seen variations of *he/she*, such as *s/he*, *he or she*, or *he/she/they*. How are readers affected by these pronouns?

        You could also investigate various forms of the alternative pronouns. Is *she or he* the same as *he or she*?

☆☆   b. Ng (1990) showed that *man* is not generic, using a release from proactive interference task. You could investigate the extent to which generic uses of terms using *man* (such as *mankind*) lead to thoughts of men. What generic alternatives are there for these terms? How is reading affected by these generic alternatives?

☆☆☆   c. Are there age differences in the interpretation of pronouns? Foertsch and Gernsbacher (1997) found that when the gender of the pronoun mismatched the stereotypical gender of the antecedent, people were slowed. That was true of college students. Does the effect hold for older adults?

        Hyde (1984) looked at first, third, and fifth grade children's interpretation of various pronouns. She found that these children knew that *he* was to be used generically but not that it could apply to both men and women. In other words, children *seem* to believe that the typical person is male. Hyde discussed this in terms of its impact on girls' self-confidence. Do children still show this pattern today? How will they interpret generic *they*?

ETHICS NOTE 8.1   Whenever you want to use a special population (like children), it will be especially difficult to get permission to conduct the research. The main problem is that children are not able to give informed consent. You will (at least) need consent from a parent. If the children are being recruited through a school, you will also need the school's permission. If you plan to use children as participants, know that your project will take longer to complete, and you should start the review process as early as possible.

☆☆   d. Is there a relationship between people's political leanings and their acceptance of *they* as a singular pronoun? For example, are conservative people more likely to be slowed by singular *they* than liberal people?

☆   e. Is there an interaction between the gender of the participant and pronoun interpretation? Langston et al. (1997) found that women and men interpreted pronouns differently. Men showed the same pattern as in Foertsch and Gernsbacher (1997). They were slowed when the pronoun mismatched the stereotypical gender of the antecedent. Women, on the other hand, were only slowed for mismatches with stereotypically feminine antecedents. They read *he* and *she* sentences at the same speed for stereotypically masculine antecedents. In other words, women seem willing to accept either gender in a stereotypically masculine profession but expect women to perform a stereotypically feminine profession. This finding suggests a number of projects.

For example, is it the case that these results reflect a change in society and not a change in pronoun interpretation? Maybe women have been made increasingly aware of other women performing what were once stereotypically masculine professions. Men, however, have not been made aware of other men performing stereotypically feminine professions. So, women are willing to broaden their expectations for a stereotypically masculine profession but maintain a narrow expectation of who will be in a stereotypically feminine profession. Men maintain narrow expectations for both. How could you test this hypothesis?

☆☆☆   f. How will training affect pronoun interpretation? Would a brief presentation on women in stereotypically masculine professions and men in stereotypically feminine professions change people's interpretations of pronouns? How much exposure to this sort of information would be required for people's reading speed to be affected?

■ ■ ■ ■ ■ ■

References

Foertsch, J., & Gernsbacher, M. A. (1997). In search of gender neutrality: Is singular *they* a cognitively efficient substitute for generic *he*? *Psychological Science, 8,* 106–111.

Gastil, J. (1990). Generic pronouns and sexist language: The oxymoronic character of masculine generics. *Sex Roles, 23,* 629–643.

Hyde, J. S. (1984). Children's understanding of sexist language. *Developmental Psychology, 20,* 697–706.

Langston, W., Ohnesorge, C., Keith, C., Scott, V., & Springer, M. (1997, May). *The effect of gender pronouns and stereotypical sex of occupations on reading time.* Poster presented at the annual meeting of the Midwestern Psychological Association, Chicago, IL.

MacKay, D. G., & Fulkerson, D. C. (1979). On the comprehension and production of pronouns. *Journal of Verbal Learning and Verbal Behavior, 18,* 661–673.

Ng, S. H. (1990). Androcentric coding of *man* and *his* in memory by language users. *Journal of Experimental Social Psychology, 26,* 455–464.

Publication Manual of the American Psychological Association (5th Ed.). (2001). Washington, DC: American Psychological Association.

9

Field Experiments

Hey, buddy, can you spare seventeen cents?

Why do people comply with some requests? Why do people say "no" to other requests? The authors of our target article for this chapter (Santos, Leve, & Pratkanis, 1994) propose that people say "no" because they develop mindless refusal scripts. They suggest that these can be disrupted by framing a request in an unusual way (the "pique technique"). In a field experiment, they showed that panhandlers generate more compliance with unusual requests (17 cents) than typical requests (a quarter).

■ ■ ■ ■ ■ ■
Introduction: Field Experiments

A field experiment involves manipulating a variable (as in an experiment) but in a natural setting. What are the benefits of conducting research in a natural setting? First, participants' behavior is more natural. Even though the experimenter may be manipulating a variable, participants are usually unaware that an observation is taking place. This allows us to take advantage of the high external validity available with observation designs. We can be reasonably sure that the behavior exhibited in our study is the same as the behavior that would ordinarily be exhibited if we were not observing.

In a field experiment, because we are manipulating a variable, we can create high internal validity and possibly even make a causal conclusion at the end of the study. However, field experiments will require you to sacrifice some of the control available in the laboratory. In the real world, it is very hard to anticipate all of the unexpected events that could arise during your observation.

A lack of control tops the list of potential problems for field experiments. In order to say conclusively that the variable you manipulated caused the changes in the dependent variable, the only thing that can differ between conditions is the manipulated variable. All of the other random events that occur in the real

METHODOLOGY NOTE 9.1   Whenever you conduct research, you want the results to be valid. Two important kinds of validity are internal and external validity. **Internal validity** has to do with the design of the experiment. If you have conducted a "clean" experiment (free from errors like confounds), then you can make a causal conclusion at the end. **External validity** (also called generalizability) has to do with your ability to extend the findings to a population. No matter how interesting your results are, if they only apply to a tiny subset of people in very specialized circumstances, they will not be very valuable. The two kinds of validity usually compete. To get high internal validity, you need control over the situation. Control makes the situation less natural, lowering external validity. To increase external validity, you give up control, lowering internal validity. Field experiments walk the line where the two kinds of validity intersect. We manipulate the situation, gaining some internal validity, but use a natural setting, preserving external validity.

world (which you cannot reasonably expect to control) will weaken your ability to attribute causality to the manipulated variable.

Another problem has to do with naturalness. Even though field experiments are conducted in a natural setting, you may be interfering with what normally takes place in that setting. This interference could have ramifications that you are not aware of. In order to ensure that your situation will *seem* natural to participants, you should always do naturalistic observation first so you are aware of the kinds of events that would ordinarily transpire in the setting.

A field experiment was used in the target article for this chapter. The researchers were interested in compliance with requests. They proposed the use of the pique technique to improve compliance. The basic idea is that when a request is unusual ("Can I borrow 17 cents?"), it disrupts refusal scripts and causes people to comply with the request.

ETHICS NOTE 9.1   Field experiment research raises special ethical considerations. For observation studies, you can make the case that you are merely observing public behavior, so you do not need to get people's permission before watching what they do. In a field experiment, however, you are intervening in the situation. When you intervene, you always raise the possibility of doing harm to the participant, and it is unfair to put people at risk without allowing them the opportunity to evaluate the risk for themselves. If you choose to conduct one of the projects in this chapter, you should carefully consider the "cost to participant" versus "knowledge to be gained" issue.

■ ■ ■ ■ ■ ■
Target Article: The Pique Technique

Why do people comply with requests? If you are interested in persuading someone to do something, this is an important question. Is it possible to identify factors that make people more likely to comply?

Two important factors were investigated by Langer, Blank, and Chanowitz (1978). (This experiment is discussed in more detail in Chapter 7.) They conducted a field experiment (their Experiment 1) to see how the wording of a request affected people's willingness to let them cut in line at the copy machine. The two factors manipulated were the size of the favor (five pages or twenty pages) and the reasonableness of the request ("because I need to make copies" or "because I'm in a rush"). Both factors turned out to be important. People were more likely to comply with small requests, and they were more likely to comply with requests that were supported by a real reason ("because I'm in a rush"). One interesting result concerned what they labeled "mindless" compliance. When the request was small, people complied just as often for a real reason as for a nonsense reason. It looks as though (for small requests) people simply comply on autopilot.

The reverse of mindless compliance is what Santos, Leve, and Pratkanis (1994) call "refusal scripts." These are a sort of mindless noncompliance, triggered by situations like that of panhandlers asking for money. Because people are already in the habit of saying "no," they can refuse to comply without paying any real attention to the request. Langer et al. (1978) showed that making a large request can disrupt mindless compliance. What could disrupt a person's refusal script? Santos et al. propose something called the pique technique. The basic idea is to disrupt a person's refusal script by framing the request in an odd way.

Santos et al.'s (1994) first experiment was a field experiment conducted on a wharf in Santa Cruz. Three female confederates of the experimenters posed as panhandlers. They approached 289 people and asked one of four questions:

1. Can you spare 17¢? (small, pique)
2. Can you spare 37¢? (large, pique)
3. Can you spare a quarter? (small, typical)
4. Can you spare any change? (large, typical)

These requests varied the amount of the request (a smaller or larger amount) and the typicality of the request (typical or pique). The experimenters expected

---

METHODOLOGY NOTE 9.2   Santos, Leve, and Pratkanis's (1994) design is a 2 × 2 between-participants factorial. Can you identify the two independent variables? What are the levels of each?

more compliance with the pique requests. The idea is that the unusual request will cause a person to think, and thinking will disrupt the refusal script.

The results supported the hypothesis. The pique requests produced a higher percentage of compliance (M = 36.6%) than the typical requests (M = 22.9%). Size of the request also mattered. Small requests (M = 36.6%) were complied with more often than large requests (M = 22.9%). Overall, the amount given did not differ based on request type.

To show that people were really thinking more in the pique conditions, the experimenters also recorded people's inquiries about the request. People in the pique conditions asked more questions (M = 11.0%) about the request than people in the typical conditions (M = 0.7%). This suggests that the pique question really does get past people's refusal script and makes them think about the request.

■ ■ ■ ■ ■ ■

Implementing the Design

Materials

You will not need any special materials for the projects in this chapter. You will probably need an observation sheet to record your results. Chapter 1 has some tips on constructing an observation sheet, and a sample sheet is presented in the supplement for Chapter 1.

Suggested Projects

☆☆ 1. You can replicate the Santos et al. (1994) experiment. Stand in front of the student union on campus and ask if you can borrow a typical amount of money or an unusual amount. Record people's rate of compliance.

2. You can make minor changes to the original design to see how the pique technique influences compliance with a range of requests.

☆☆   a. Instead of asking for an amount that is unusual, you could justify the request with an unusual reason. For example, a group of students at Middle Tennessee State University requested either 5 cents or 25 cents, and justified the request by saying "to call someone" or "to call my therapist." The hypothesis (based on the pique technique) is that people will be more likely to comply if the justification is unusual.

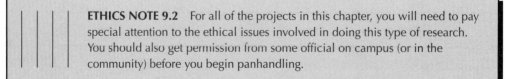

ETHICS NOTE 9.2   For all of the projects in this chapter, you will need to pay special attention to the ethical issues involved in doing this type of research. You should also get permission from some official on campus (or in the community) before you begin panhandling.

☆☆☆   b. You can vary what you are asking for. A different group of Middle Tennessee State University students prepared a long survey (approximately eight pages). Then, they asked people on campus if they would mind completing "a couple of pages of this survey" or completing "2 and 1/8 pages of this survey." They expected that people would be more likely to comply with the "2 and 1/8" question. But they also expected that, with the pique question, people would be more likely to fulfill the exact request. In other words, more people may comply with a pique request, but the amount of compliance may also be exactly what was asked for. In a way, this is a hidden cost of the pique technique. Overall, you may get a higher response rate, but the amount you get from each person is smaller because he or she will give you exactly what you asked for.

☆☆☆   c. What about the amount of the favor? While it is true that 37 cents is more than 17 cents, it is not a lot more. Can you incorporate larger amounts and a greater variety of amounts (maybe a range from a quarter to five dollars)? What happens at really large amounts? How high does the amount have to be before the pique technique stops working?

■ ■ ■ ■ ■ ■
References

Langer, E., Blank, A., & Chanowitz, B. (1978). The mindlessness of ostensibly thoughtful action: The role of "placebic" information in interpersonal interaction. *Journal of Personality and Social Psychology, 36,* 635–642.

Santos, M. D., Leve, C., & Pratkanis, A. R. (1994). Hey buddy, can you spare seventeen cents? Mindful persuasion and the pique technique. *Journal of Applied Social Psychology, 24,* 755–764. Used with permission of the author.

Part Three

Advanced Experimental Methodology

The research techniques in Part Three involve combining the results of multiple experiments to focus in on the answers to research questions. Strong inference is used when there are several competing explanations for a phenomenon; the purpose of the strong inference technique is to rule out incorrect explanations. The final chapter discusses ways to combine both correlational and experimental techniques into a research program.

Strong Inference

How do blind people "see"?

You have probably seen a blind person negotiate a cluttered environment with the assistance of a cane or a guide dog. The target article for this chapter investigates a more difficult situation: How do blind people negotiate an unfamiliar environment without external assistance? In one set of studies, the authors establish that blind people can detect obstacles in unfamiliar environments. A carefully designed series of experiments shows that this is done using auditory feedback.

■ ■ ■ ■ ■ ■
Introduction: Falsification—"Incrementing by Exclusion"

The purpose of this chapter is to tie together some of the leftover issues from Parts One and Two. The first issue is: How do you combine a series of studies into a research program? As you have probably seen by now, the research enterprise is cumulative. New studies build on old studies; research is conducted as part of a larger program of investigation. How do studies relate to one another?

The second issue has to do with falsification. You have probably heard that you can never prove anything true, but you can prove something false. Given that, how do we make progress? For example, how do we decide that a particular therapy is valid if we cannot prove it true? If we prove everything false, what is left?

The solution for both issues is **strong inference**. At its core, strong inference works like statistical hypothesis testing. You set up a group of mutually exclusive and exhaustive hypotheses and then attempt to rule out all but one of those hypotheses. The difference is that we are getting our hypotheses from theories that exist to explain the phenomenon of interest. We can have as many hypotheses as there are theories.

The steps in strong inference (Platt, 1964):

1. Devise multiple hypotheses. You can do this based on your own intuitions (not optimal) or based on a careful review of the literature (much better). The goal is to gather together all proposed answers to your question of interest.
2. Design a study to test between these alternatives. Ideally, each possible outcome of the study will be consistent with only one of your alternatives and inconsistent with all of the rest.
3. Carry out your research. Use the techniques covered in Parts One and Two.
1′. Repeat the procedure. Sometimes, you repeat these steps several times to get to just one hypothesis. This might happen if you cannot force all of the hypotheses to make different predictions or if you realize after the study that a slightly different version of one of the hypotheses might still be OK, and you want to refine it even more. This process is similar to tournament bowling: The two lowest contenders meet. The winner advances to meet the next highest contender. The winner of that round advances. . . .

Using strong inference offers two main benefits. First, it protects you from your bias to try to confirm your first idea. Instead, you are forced to think about all of the possibilities. You can see confirmation biases at work on some TV game shows. For example, in *What's My Line?* a celebrity panel had to guess the identity of a mystery guest. As the panel got some idea of who the guest was, the questions could become very specific, such as "Do you have a new picture coming out where you play a brunette divorcée living in Manhattan?" If the answer was "yes," then the person was identified, but if the answer was "no," little had been gained. The purpose of the question was to confirm a preexisting hypothesis. If that hypothesis was wrong, then the questioner was stumped.

You can feel your own confirmation bias in the following example (taken from Wason, 1960, as described in Myers, 1995). I have a rule in mind that generated this sequence of numbers: "2, 4, 6." Try to think of my rule. When you have it, generate your own sequence and write it down. At this point, if we were in the room together, you could ask me if your sequence fits my rule. Chances are it would, because most people come up with sequences that involve counting up by twos. In other words, people make the leap from their hypothesized rule to a sequence that fits it. That can confirm their first guess, but it cannot show that that guess is wrong. In this case, the rule is any three numbers that go up. So, "123, 1000, 1001" would fit just as well as "20, 22, 24." If you try only to confirm, there is no way for you to find that out. The results of your confirmation experiment would convince you that you were right when, in fact, you were wrong.

A second benefit of strong inference is the speed with which you can make progress in answering questions. By ruling out incorrect hypotheses, you can avoid wasting time investigating something that is wrong. For example, we may have several competing theories of depression. If we can rule out all but one, then we may develop the most appropriate therapy based on that one theory. We have incremented our knowledge of depression by getting rid of all of the hypotheses that are wrong.

Our target article will apply the strong inference procedure to explanations of the ability of blind people to navigate in an unfamiliar environment.

■ ■ ■ ■ ■ ■
Target Article: Obstacle Detection by the Blind

How can a blind person move through an unfamiliar environment without walking into anything? There are several hypotheses to explain how this might be possible (Crafts, Schneirla, Robinson, & Gilbert, 1950).

1. *Occult*. Blind people have honed a sixth sense that we all possess but that sighted people ignore or cannot use properly. Blind people use this sixth sense to navigate in unfamiliar environments.
2. *Facial vision*. Blind people are able to sense changes in the air currents moving around their faces, and they use this information to avoid obstacles.
3. *Auditory*. Blind people pay attention to sounds (such as footfalls) as they reflect off things in the environment. They use this information to avoid obstacles.

Crafts et al. (1950) used a strong inference procedure to determine which of these hypotheses can be ruled out.

Experiments 1–3

The goal of the first set of experiments was to establish a methodology for investigating the phenomenon. The researchers wanted to determine if blind people really could avoid obstacles, and they wanted to work out a way to assess obstacle detection ability.

The participants were two blind people and two sighted people. All four participants wore blindfolds during all of the experiments. The basic methodology was to position the participant in a hall and tell him to approach the wall at the other end. The experimenters measured three things:

1. *Distance perception*. How far away could participants detect the wall?
2. *Close perception*. How close could participants get without hitting the wall?
3. *Number of collisions*. How many times did participants hit the wall before completing 25 successful trials?

The experimenters used two basic conditions: Hard shoes on a hard floor and socks on carpet.

Experiment 1 established that blind participants were good obstacle detectors and that sighted participants were not as good. In three sets of trials (two on the hard floor and one on carpet), the blind participants had an average distance perception of 10.36 feet, an average close perception of 0.59 feet, and an average of 1.0 collision per set of 25 successful trials. All of the collisions were in the carpeted condition. The sighted participants had an average distance perception of 2.08 feet, an average close perception of 0.76 feet, and an average of 8.5 collisions per set of 25 successful trials. The sighted participants did show remarkable improvement with practice. In the first round, they had an average of 17.0 collisions. In the third round, they had an average of 3.5 collisions. Note that the high number of collisions makes their close perception score a little less impressive. They did get pretty close when they failed to collide, but they also collided a lot, suggesting that they did not really know where the wall was. This was especially true in the early going.

In Experiment 2 the experimenters refined the methodology by using a movable screen as an obstacle. In Experiment 1, the blind participants had an advantage because they showed much better orientation ability in the hall. They were able to walk in a straight line without assistance and were not confused by being spun around before each trial. To compensate for this, participants always started at the same spot in Experiment 2, and a movable screen was used as the obstacle. This way, even if the blind participants knew exactly where they were in the hall, they could know the screen's location only if they actually detected it.

In Experiment 3 the experimenters substituted thicker carpeting. The experimenters also incorporated some catch trials where there was no screen. This was done to ensure that participants were really detecting the obstacle and not just guessing, especially for distance perception. Finally, the experimenters varied both the starting point and the screen position to make it harder for participants to use orientation ability in the task.

These experiments showed three things. First, blind participants located obstacles very well, so there was a phenomenon worthy of investigating with additional experiments. Second, the experiments established a nice methodology for investigating obstacle detection. Extraneous factors such as guessing and blind people's superior orienting ability could be ruled out. What was left was a measure of "pure" obstacle detection. Third, the experiments showed that with just a little practice sighted participants could become nearly as good as blind participants at detecting obstacles. This allowed the experimenters to eliminate the "occult" hypothesis (it is unlikely that some latent sixth sense could be activated so quickly).

Experiment 4

The fourth experiment was designed to determine if the ability to feel air currents on one's skin is necessary to detect obstacles. The experimenters repeated Experiment 3, but put a heavy felt hood over the participants' heads and heavy gloves on their hands. Then, with no air currents, participants tried to detect the obstacle. If the facial vision hypothesis were correct, participants would have had a very difficult time in this condition. Because they were expected to need air currents to detect obstacles, and they did not have air currents, they should not have been able to detect anything. On the other hand, if the auditory hypothesis were correct, participants should have done reasonably well in this task. Their ears were relatively unaffected by the hood and gloves.

The results were that participants' perceptions were a bit worse, but not as bad as they should have been if the participants *had to* have air currents to detect obstacles. Combining one set of hard floor trials and one set of carpet trials, blind participants had an average distance perception of 6.10 feet, an average close perception of 0.61 feet, and an average of 2.8 collisions per set of trials. Sighted participants had an average distance perception of 2.20 feet, an average close perception of 0.80 feet, and an average of 2.8 collisions per set of trials. The conclusion was that feeling air currents on one's skin is not necessary for obstacle detection.

Experiment 5

At this point, we could say that only the auditory hypothesis is left. The first set of studies ruled out the occult hypothesis, and Experiment 4 ruled out the facial vision hypothesis. We have completed the three steps in the strong inference process. We listed three hypotheses, designed experiments in which each hypothesis made a different prediction, and carried out the experiments until only one hypothesis was left.

We now come to step 1′. Can either of the eliminated hypotheses be modified so that it might still be a contender? The facial vision hypothesis might. We have shown that air currents are not necessary for obstacle detection. However, air currents might still be sufficient (you do not have to have them, but if they are all you do have, you can do the task).

Crafts et al. (1950) needed a new experiment that would allow them to find out if participants could do the task with just exposed skin but no auditory feedback. In Experiment 5, the experimenters masked all of the sounds with ear plugs. The participants' faces and hands were exposed, allowing them to feel any air currents that might enable them to detect obstacles. In this case, the prediction from the facial vision hypothesis would be that performance would be very good (all of the skin needed to detect obstacles was exposed). The prediction from the auditory hypothesis would be really poor performance. Without the ability to hear sounds reflected off the screen, participants should be unable to detect it.

There are no results to report from this experiment because, without auditory feedback, participants could not do the task at all. Out of 100 trials, no participant *ever* detected the screen. So, feeling air currents was not sufficient. The experimenters eliminated the modified version of the facial vision hypothesis.

The series of experiments is summed up in Figure 10.1. The experimenters started with multiple hypotheses, performed an organized series of experiments to test between them, and repeated the steps until just one hypothesis was left.

Figure 10.1 How experiments combine to rule out hypotheses.
    Source: Derived from a figure used by William Epstein in his Research Methods lectures, used by permission of William Epstein.

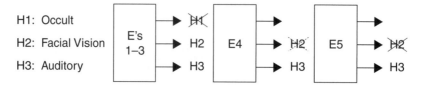

H1: Occult

H2: Facial Vision

H3: Auditory

■■■■■■
Implementing the Design

Materials

The projects suggested below are based on each of the chapters in Parts One and Two. Any materials you need will be described with those chapters.

Suggested Projects

Strong inference can be used to address any research question where there are two or more competing hypotheses. The projects below suggest a pair of hypotheses to explain some aspect of the studies described in Parts One and Two. Do not feel limited to these questions. Any time there are multiple hypotheses, you can carry out a strong inference study. Ask yourself: "Are there alternative explanations?" and "How can I test between them?"

☆☆   1. Ruback and Juieng (1997) were concerned that people may take longer to back out of a parking space when someone is waiting because of distraction and not territoriality. Having someone waiting makes the situation more dangerous, so it is reasonable to slow down for safety. How could you test between the safety hypothesis and the territoriality hypothesis? What observations could you collect?

☆☆☆   2. Who is responsible for grade inflation? Did students force faculty to give higher grades by evaluating hard-grading faculty more harshly? Or did faculty lower their standards and start to give higher grades for average work? Design a study to see where the pressure for grade inflation is coming from.

☆☆☆   3. Beck and Katcher (1984) suggest that the benefits of pet-facilitated therapy arise from the human interactions that accompany bringing the pets to nursing homes, and the like. So, it is not pets that improve people's attitudes, it is people that improve people's attitudes. How could you test between these two alternatives?

☆☆   4. A number of alternative explanations of Stroop interference were proposed in Chapter 4. We will just consider two here. It may be that having a specific interference slows people down (two different colors in mind at once), or it may be that having any interference slows people down (like having two representations of the same color). Design an experiment to test between these alternatives.

☆☆☆ 5. Frick-Horbury and Guttentag (1998) proposed that imagining gestures may be what is beneficial for word retrieval, not actual gestures. But they never presented any evidence for this hypothesis. Can you design an experiment to determine if it is imagined or actual gestures that facilitate word retrieval?

☆☆☆ 6. Pressey (1921) suggests that people change their behavior in colored environments because they know they are supposed to, based on cultural stereotypes about various colors (e.g., that red is arousing). Design an experiment to determine whether physiological arousal in red rooms is due to the color or to people's cultural expectations.

☆☆☆ 7. Niedenthal and Setterlund (1994) showed that mood influences perception. How does it do this? One way to test this would be to work out a model similar to the one Sternberg (1969) created for short-term memory search. To respond to a word in lexical decision tasks you have to encode it, make a decision, and respond. Mood could affect one or all of these stages. For example, it could affect encoding by slightly boosting the activation of every item with which it is associated (a sad mood makes all sad words a little more accessible). Or, it may affect the decision stage (e.g., words are encoded just as quickly regardless of mood, but it is easier to decide about words that match the current mood). Can you design an experiment to tease apart the contribution of each stage to the overall decision time?

☆☆☆ 8. Foertsch and Gernsbacher (1997) claim that *they* is a good substitute for *he*. But it may be that their participants were able to figure out the design of the experiment. Knowing that mismatching pronouns should take longer, participants deliberately slowed down for mismatching clauses. For matching and *they* clauses, participants read normally. Can you test between a "cognitively efficient *they*" hypothesis and a demand characteristics hypothesis?

☆☆☆ 9. Santos, Leve, and Pratkanis (1994) claim that an unusual request disrupts mindless refusal scripts and makes a person more likely to respond. An alternative explanation is that an unusual request makes a beggar seem more threatening, and people are more likely to comply due to heightened arousal. My thinking goes something like this: People are already uncomfortable being approached by a panhandler. When that panhandler seems a little odd, they comply to make the panhandler go away more quickly. Can you devise an experiment to test between the two hypotheses?

☆☆☆ 10. Now that we know that blind people detect obstacles using auditory information, we can try to figure out which aspects of the auditory information help them to do it. The authors of the original study investigated this by contrasting the *intensity* (volume) of the sound with the *frequency* (pitch) of the sound. Design an experiment that will allow you to determine which of these characteristics allows for improved obstacle detection.

■ ■ ■ ■ ■ ■

References

Beck, A. M., & Katcher, A. H. (1984). A new look at pet-facilitated therapy. *Journal of the American Veterinary Medical Association, 184,* 414–421.

Crafts, L. W., Schneirla, T. C., Robinson, E. E., & Gilbert, R. W. (1950). *Recent experiments in psychology* (2nd ed., pp. 137–169). New York: McGraw-Hill.

Foertsch, J., & Gernsbacher, M. A. (1997). In search of gender neutrality: Is singular *they* a cognitively efficient substitute for generic *he*? *Psychological Science, 8,* 106–111.

Frick-Horbury, D., & Guttentag, R. E. (1998). The effects of restricting hand gesture production on lexical retrieval and free recall. *American Journal of Psychology, 111,* 43–62.

Myers, D. G. (1995). *Psychology* (4th Ed.). New York: Worth.

Niedenthal, P. M., & Setterlund, M. B. (1994). Emotion congruence in perception. *Personality and Social Psychology Bulletin, 20,* 401–411.

Platt, J. R. (1964). Strong inference. *Science, 146,* 347–353.

Pressey, S. L. (1921). The influence of color upon mental and motor efficiency. *American Journal of Psychology, 32,* 326–356.

Ruback, R. B., & Juieng, D. (1997). Territorial defense in parking lots: Retaliation against waiting drivers. *Journal of Applied Social Psychology, 27,* 821–834.

Santos, M. D., Leve, C., & Pratkanis, A. R. (1994). Hey buddy, can you spare seventeen cents? Mindful persuasion and the pique technique. *Journal of Applied Social Psychology, 24,* 755–764.

Sternberg, S. (1969). The discovery of processing stages: Extensions of Donders' method. *Acta Psychologica, 30,* 276–315.

Wason, P. C. (1960). On the failure to eliminate hypotheses in a conceptual task. *Quarterly Journal of Experimental Psychology, 12,* 129–140.

CHAPTER 11

Combining Correlation Research and Experiments

Are depressed people "sadder but wiser"?

Does a perceived lack of control over the environment cause depression (as in the learned helplessness theory), or does depression cause people to more accurately perceive how much control they have? This chapter summarizes a set of correlation studies exploring the relationship between depression and judged control (Alloy & Abramson, 1979). The chapter also summarizes an experiment that determined the causal direction of the relationship (Alloy, Abramson, & Viscusi, 1981). It appears that changes in mood cause changes in perception of control.

■ ■ ■ ■ ■ ■
Introduction: "Correlation Does Not Imply Causation"

This chapter continues with the theme of combining studies into a research program. The purpose is to look at how correlation research can be used in conjunction with experiments to answer research questions. The approach outlined below is to use correlation research for exploration and hypothesis generation and then use experiments to test the hypotheses that are generated. By combining the two, a researcher can take advantage of the benefits of both.

By now, you have probably memorized the expression "correlation does not imply causation." Even if the correlation between two variables is large (whether positive or negative), indicating that a strong relationship exists, it is not possible to say that one of the variables caused changes in the other. To say that one variable caused changes in another, we need to manipulate that variable and randomly assign participants to conditions. In other words, we need to do an experiment.

Our target article for this chapter combined correlation research with an experiment to make a conclusion about causality. The first set of studies were correlational. The researchers investigated the relationship between depression and perceived control. The final study reports the results of an experiment in which mood was manipulated to determine its effect on perceived control.

■ ■ ■ ■ ■ ■

Target Article: Combining Correlational and Experimental Approaches: Depression and Judged Control

Finding a Correlation Between Depression and Judged Control

The first set of studies were conducted by Alloy and Abramson (1979). The research was motivated, in part, by the "learned helplessness" theory. Seligman and Maier (1967) demonstrated that when dogs learn in one situation that they cannot escape from an electric shock, they do not try to escape in new situations where escape is possible. Research with humans demonstrated that they exhibit similar behavior when exposed to an uncontrollable noise (Gatchel, Paulus, & Maples, 1975). In general, when there is no contingency between responses and outcomes, organisms (including humans) stop trying to control the situation. Gatchel et al. also found that "helpless" participants exhibit symptoms of depression. So, the learned helplessness theory can loosely be described as "helplessness leads to depression."

Alloy and Abramson (1979) developed a task that allowed them to manipulate the contingency between a response and an outcome. The response was pressing a button, and the outcome was a green light coming on. For each trial of the study, participants either did or did not press the button. Then, the light either came on or it did not. In other words, there were four things that could happen:

1. Press, and the light comes on.
2. Press, and the light does not come on.
3. Do not press, and the light comes on.
4. Do not press, and the light does not come on.

Participants in a study could have complete control over the green light, no control over the green light, or intermediate control. For complete control, every time the button was pressed, the light came on. Every time the button was not pressed, the light did not come on. For no control, there was no relationship between pressing and the light coming on (for all intents and purposes, the button was not even hooked up to the light).

> **METHODOLOGY NOTE 11.1** I am intentionally blurring the distinction between quasi experiments and correlation studies in the description of the target article (this distinction is discussed more fully in Chapter 3). Even though our target article for this section will be using a quasi-experimental design, the authors will not be able to make conclusions about causality. Unless an independent variable is *manipulated* by the experimenter, the limits of correlation research still apply.

Based on learned helplessness theory, Alloy and Abramson (1979) expected that depressed participants would be poor at estimating their control over the light. Because they have learned that their actions have little impact on the environment, they should systematically underestimate their amount of control. On the other hand, nondepressed participants should be reasonably accurate at assessing control. Alloy and Abramson conducted several studies to test these predictions.

■ Study 1

Alloy and Abramson (1979) defined control as the percentage of time the light came on for presses minus the percentage of time the light came on for no presses. Here are some examples of varying degrees of control:

1. For 100% control, the light should come on 100% of the time for presses and 0% of the time for no presses. 100% – 0% = 100% control.
2. For 0% control, the light should come on equally often for presses or no presses. For example, the light might come on 75% of the time for presses and 75% of the time for no presses. 75% – 75% = 0%.
3. For intermediate control, the percentages should vary. For example, if the light comes on for 75% of presses and 25% of no presses, it would yield 50% control. 75% – 25% = 50%.

Alloy and Abramson (1979) had three levels of control:

1. The 75–50 problem had 75% light for presses and 50% light for no presses. 75% – 50% = 25% control.
2. The 75–25 problem had 50% control.
3. The 75–0 problem had 75% control.

The participants were 24 depressed females, 24 nondepressed females, 24 depressed males, and 24 nondepressed males.

Contrary to the prediction, depressed people did not underestimate control relative to nondepressed people. Both groups were accurate at estimating control, especially for the 75–25 and 75–0 problems. The results of this study indicated that depressed people could accurately estimate control when they had control.

■ Study 2

The participants in Study 2 had no control. The question was: Can depressed and nondepressed individuals accurately assess a *lack of* control? There were two problems:

1. The 75–75 problem had 0% control; the light came on 75% of the time.
2. The 25–25 problem had 0% control, but the light came on 25% of the time.

The only difference between the problems was how frequently the light came on. Alloy and Abramson (1979) were concerned that the frequency with which the light came on would influence the judgment. Because getting the light to come on might be perceived as a positive event, Alloy and Abramson thought participants might overestimate control for the 75–75 problem (where the light came on a lot) but not be eager to claim control in the 25–25 problem (where the light only came on 25% of the time). Note that the true amount of control was 0% in both cases.

The participants were 16 depressed females, 16 nondepressed females, 16 depressed males, and 16 nondepressed males.

Alloy and Abramson (1979) found that depressed participants were relatively accurate for both problems (estimating about 10% control). The nondepressed participants overestimated control in the 75–75 problem (claiming about 40% control), but not in the 25–25 problem. In other words, nondepressed people suffer from an "illusion of control" when good things happen but are otherwise accurate.

■ Study 3

For Study 3, the valence of the outcome was explicitly manipulated. There were two problems:

1. 50–50 WIN. There was 0% control, but participants received 25¢ each time the light came on for a total of $5.00 by the end of the study.
2. 50–50 LOSE. There was 0% control. Participants started with a balance of $5.00. They lost 25¢ each time the light did not come on for a total loss of $5.00.

Note that for both problems, no matter what participants did, they either won or lost $5.00. Alloy and Abramson (1979) expected nondepressed participants to claim control in the WIN problem but not in the LOSE problem.

The participants were 16 depressed females, 16 nondepressed females, 16 depressed males, and 16 nondepressed males.

Nondepressed participants overestimated control in the WIN problem (around 60%) but not in the LOSE problem (around 20%, equal to nondepressed participants).

The conclusion: Depressed people are accurate at assessing control in situations where they have control and in situations where they have no control. Nondepressed people are accurate when they have control but overestimate control when they have no control and good things happen. As Alloy and Abramson (1979) put it, depressed people are "sadder but wiser" (p. 479).

An Experiment to Determine Causal Relationships

At this point, we have a correlation between depression and judgment of control. Overall, depressed people are more accurate at assessing control than nondepressed people. What we do not know is whether depression causes accurate judgment of control or whether accurate judgment of control causes depression. Also, some third factor could cause both depression and accurate control. Alloy and Abramson (1979) say in the discussion that "a crucial question is whether depression itself leads people to be 'realistic' or whether realistic people are more vulnerable to depression" (p. 480).

The answer to this question can be determined with an experiment that manipulates mood. If people who are assigned to a sad mood become more accurate at assessing control, we will know that mood causes changes in perceived control. That is the purpose of the second set of studies.

The experiment was conducted by Alloy, Abramson, and Viscusi (1981). Alloy et al. state the problem this way: "Perhaps the state of depression itself causes people to accurately assess their impact on events . . . alternatively, those people who tend to judge accurately how much control they have over outcomes may be more vulnerable to depressive states . . . [or] some third variable such as anhedonia or attributional style may be responsible for both" (p. 1130).

Alloy et al. (1981) used the Velten mood induction procedure (Velten, 1968) to induce either a sad mood (D-Ind), a neutral mood (D-Neu or ND-Neu), or an elated mood (E-Ind). (In the article's terminology, D = depressed, E = elated, ND = nondepressed, Ind = induced, Neu = neutral, and Sim = simulated.) The procedure for inducing mood involved reading statements that should produce the correct mood. Example statements are "things will be better and better today" for elation and "I want to go to sleep and never wake up" for depression. The participants then performed the 50–50 WIN problem from Alloy and Abramson (1979) and estimated the amount of control they had over the green light.

There were 40 depressed female participants. Of these, 10 were induced to elation (E-Ind), 10 were induced to a neutral mood (D-Neu), and 10 were left alone (D-No). In addition, 10 were instructed to simulate a person in the E-Ind group. In other words, they were pretending that they had been manipulated into an elated mood. This was the E-Sim group.

There were also 40 nondepressed female participants. Of these, 10 were induced to depression (D-Ind), 10 were induced to a neutral mood (ND-Neu), and 10 were left alone (ND-No). There were also 10 D-Sim participants who pretended they had been induced to depression.

METHODOLOGY NOTE 11.2 The design of Alloy, Abramson, and Viscusi's (1981) study is a 2 × 4 between-participants factorial. The first independent variable is direction of mood (down from the present mood state or up from the present mood state). The second independent variable is mood manipulation (induced to a mood, simulated a mood, neutral mood induction, and no mood induction). There will be eight groups in the experiment. Note that because the design is between participants, 80 people had to be run. Why were Alloy et al. unable to take advantage of a within-participants design?

> **METHODOLOGY NOTE 11.3**   Alloy, Abramson, and Viscusi (1981) have included three control groups in each condition. One control group (Sim) allows them to rule out the hypothesis that pretending to be in a mood will be sufficient. Another control group (Neu) allows them to rule out the possibility that the act of flipping through the cards causes the changes, regardless of the mood. The third control group allows for comparison to participants who have not been treated at all. Using multiple control groups allows Alloy et al. to rule out several confounds within the context of a single experiment.

The two groups of primary interest are the depressed participants induced to elation (E-Ind) and the nondepressed participants induced to depression (D-Ind). If the elation-induced participants overestimate control as much as the nondepressed control group, that would suggest that changing a person's mood changes his or her perception of control. Similarly, if the depression-induced participants are as accurate as the depressed control group, that would also show that changing mood changes perception of control. The findings are illustrated in Figure 11.1 (redrawn from Figure 3 of Alloy et al., 1981).

The participants induced to elation (E-Ind) overestimated control as much as the nondepressed control group (ND-No). The participants induced to depression (D-Ind) were as accurate as the depressed control group (D-No). So, changing people's moods appears to have caused their perception of control to change.

Figure 11.1 Judged control as a function of condition.
Source: From "Induced mood and the illusion of control," by L. B. Alloy, L. Y. Abramson, and D. Viscusi, 1981, *Journal of Personality and Social Psychology, 41,* pp. 1129–1140. Copyright © 1981 by the American Psychological Association. Reprinted with permission.

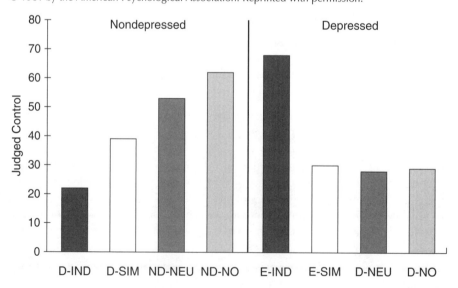

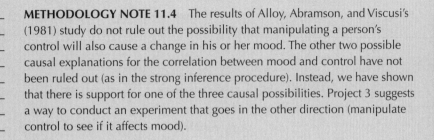

METHODOLOGY NOTE 11.4   The results of Alloy, Abramson, and Viscusi's (1981) study do not rule out the possibility that manipulating a person's control will also cause a change in his or her mood. The other two possible causal explanations for the correlation between mood and control have not been ruled out (as in the strong inference procedure). Instead, we have shown that there is support for one of the three causal possibilities. Project 3 suggests a way to conduct an experiment that goes in the other direction (manipulate control to see if it affects mood).

We can now answer the question we started with: Does accurate perception of control cause depression, or does depression cause accurate perception of control? We know that depression (or mood) is likely to cause a change in perception of control.

Implementing the Design

Materials

To manipulate mood, you can use the Velten mood induction procedure described in Chapter 7. Other mood induction procedures are also described in Chapter 7.

The control task can be implemented with the *Judged Control Task* software. You will also need the *JCT Analysis* software to prepare your data for statistical analysis.

If you do not have access to a computer, the projects could also be implemented in a paper-and-pencil format. Make two cards, one with a picture of a light bulb (or the word "yes," or some other variation). The other card should be blank (or have the word "no," or the like). You will need a button or buzzer that the participant can use to produce a response. You will also need a stopwatch to time the events and a score sheet to keep track of responses.

Use a random number table to form a sequence of feedback for "press" responses and a sequence for "no-press" responses. If you plan on 40 trials, have enough feedback for 40 press and 40 no-press responses. To construct a feedback sequence, decide on the percentage of feedback you want to use. For example, if I want 25% feedback for press responses, I would look for the numbers 1, 2, 3, and 4 in my random number table. For each 1 encountered, I would give feedback indicating that the light came on. For the other three numbers, I would give light-off feedback. Once I had 40 responses, I would make sure that exactly 25% had light-on feedback. I would repeat this step for the no-press response sequence. You can also use the *Randomize Numbers* software utility to randomize your feedback sequences.

To present the task, ask the participant for a response, wait until the time elapses, and present the correct feedback. For example, if on the first trial the participant does not press, and the light is not supposed to come on for the first no press, hold up the blank card. Continue in this way until all of the trials are presented. Make several feedback sequences to avoid any potential confounds related to the feedback order.

■ The *Judged Control Task* Software

The software re-creates the equipment used by Alloy and Abramson (1979). You can use the software by running the standard settings, or you can customize the software to present your own design. Rudimentary help is provided within the software, but you will still need to read the original research carefully to understand all of the components of the task. This is especially true if you plan to create your own settings. Follow the installation instructions in Appendix E to install the software from the CD.

❏ *Running a Study That Is Already Set Up*

To use Alloy and Abramson's (1979) problems, open the "Standard Experiment Problems" folder and double-click the problem you want. The problems are:

1. 75–50 problem; 75–25 problem; 75–0 problem. These allow you to replicate the three conditions in Study 1 of Alloy and Abramson (1979).
2. 75–75 problem; 25–25 problem. These allow you to replicate the conditions of Study 2 of Alloy and Abramson (1979).
3. 50–50 WIN; 50–50 LOSE. These allow you to replicate the conditions of Study 3 of Alloy and Abramson (1979) and the experiment in Alloy et al. (1981).

If you run a standard problem, the program will automatically load the correct parameters. All you need to do is enter a participant number and indicate whether the participant is male or female and depressed or not depressed. If you want to implement more complicated designs (such as the experiment by Alloy et al., 1981), use blocks of participant numbers for each condition. For example, 1 through 10 = E-Sim, 11 through 20 = E-Ind, and so on. That will allow you to code these conditions for analysis when the time comes.

For the standard problems, the computer will automatically present instructions and collect data on all of the dependent measures used by Alloy and Abramson (1979). You might want to be present during the instruction phase so the participant can ask questions. The participants will have the option of saving their data after the study. For analysis purposes, all of the participant data files need to be saved into the same folder, and they all need to be named "JCTP#," where "#" is the participant number entered at the beginning of the study.

❏ *Setting Up a Study*

To program your own study, double-click the *Judged Control Task* program. When the program is running, click the "Set Up" button. This will take you to the program's parameter screen. You can modify an existing problem by loading it from this screen.

There are three types of parameters that you will need to set before running a study. Presentation parameters tell the program how to control the presentation. Task parameters tell the program which task to use in the study. Dependent variable parameters tell the program which dependent variables to present. Each will be discussed in turn.

Setting the presentation parameters   Click the "Change" button by "Presentation Parameters." You will get the screen in Figure 11.2.

Figure 11.2 *Judged Control Task* presentation parameters screen.

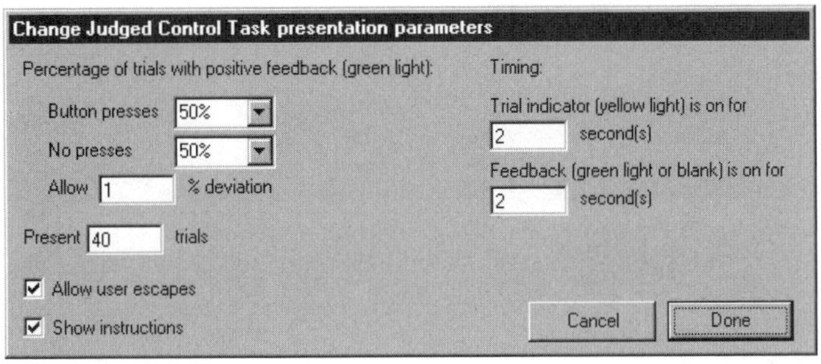

You can change the percentage of reinforcement for presses and no presses. The available settings are 0%, 25%, 50%, 75%, and 100%. You can also enter the amount by which the true percentages can deviate from your targets.

The program will randomly choose a response for the first five trials. After that it will continue to choose at random but try to maintain your percentages. Sometimes it will get into a pattern when it is doing this (e.g., light, no light, light, no light . . .). To avoid this, you can allow it to deviate slightly from the true percentages. As long as the deviation is low, your final feedback percentages will match your settings. Run yourself as a subject through the program several times when you are setting up a problem to see how it works.

You can allow the user to exit the program early. Windows users will have an "Escape" button on the screen. Macintosh users will exit by clicking the mouse button when the yellow light is on. This feature is useful if you are evaluating your settings to see if the program is working properly. It is dangerous to leave this feature on during data collection, because one accidental button click can prematurely stop the program.

If "Show instructions" is checked, the standard instructions will be presented. You might choose not to show instructions if you prefer to read the instructions to the participant. Reading the instructions will offer more opportunities for the participant to ask questions and fully understand the task.

You can change the number of trials. You should have at least 20 to make the actual percentages match your settings. The more trials you have, the more likely it is that the percentages will be correct.

You can adjust the timing. The duration of the lights and the press interval can be as short as one second or as long as you would like. Windows users will not be able to set a press interval. Instead, Windows users will click "Click

Button" to press and "Wait" to not press. There is no time limit for choosing this response.

When you finish with these settings, click "Done" to return to the parameters screen.

Setting the task parameters   Click the "Change" button by "Task Parameters." You will get the screen in Figure 11.3.

Figure 11.3 *Judged Control Task* task parameters screen.

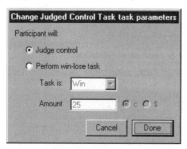

The task can be judgment or win–lose. If you choose a win–lose task, you can enter the amount to be won or lost on each trial. For win–lose problems, the press and no press percentages should be equal.

When you finish with these settings, click "Done" to return to the parameters screen.

Setting the dependent variable parameters   Click the "Change" button by "Dependent Variable Parameters." You will get the screen in Figure 11.4.

Figure 11.4 *Judged Control Task* dependent variables screen.

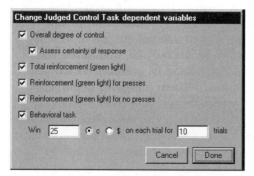

You can collect data for all of the variables used by Alloy and Abramson (1979), or you can turn some or all of them off. This allows you to control the dependent measures if you want to include your own. If you collect no dependent measures, no data will be saved, so you should be sure to write the problem type and other information on your own data sheet. When you finish with these settings, click "Done" to return to the parameters screen.

Your current settings for all of the parameters will be displayed verbally on the master parameters screen. This screen will allow you to save your current settings. Double-clicking your problem will launch the program and automatically load your settings.

■ The *JCT Analysis* Software

When you finish collecting data, you will need to analyze it using the *JCT Analysis* software. You can view the results for a single participant or prepare a file with the results of an entire study. You will have to run the data files through the analysis program before you will be able to view the results.

❏ *Viewing a Participant's Data File*

To print a single participant's results, double-click that participant's data file. You will see the screen in Figure 11.5.

Figure 11.5 *JCT Analysis* output screen.

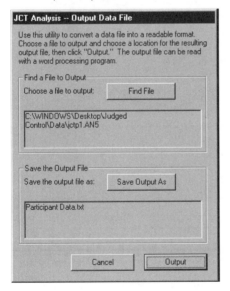

If you double-clicked a data file, you can click "Output," and the data will be processed. The file that is created will be saved in the same folder as the data file and will be called "Participant Data." Double-clicking the output file will allow you to see the results for that participant. If the analysis program is already running, chose "Output Data File" from the main window to get this screen. (Macintosh users will choose actions from the "Analysis Menu" in the menu bar.) Choose "Find File" to choose a file to print. Click "Save Output As" to create a file for the processed data. You will be asked to choose a name and location for the data file. Macintosh users have the option of sending a file to the printer, but this option may not always work correctly.

❏ *Analyzing a Group of Data Files*

If you double-click the *JCT Analysis* program and choose "Analyze Data" from the main screen, you will get the screen in Figure 11.6. (Macintosh users will choose actions from the "Analysis Menu" in the menu bar.)

Figure 11.6 *JCT Analysis* analysis screen.

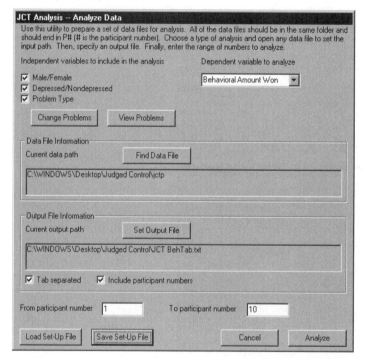

The principle job of the analysis part of the program is to sort the data for statistical packages. This will allow replication of the analyses reported in Alloy and Abramson (1979). Analysis set-up information will consist of:

1. *Independent variables to include in the analysis.* You can sort the data into three categories:
   a. *Male/female.* If you select this option, the first column in the data file will have a 1 for males and a 2 for females.
   b. *Depressed/nondepressed.* If you select this option the second column in the data file will have a 1 for depressed participants and a 2 for nondepressed participants.
   c. *Problem type.* If you select this option, you will be asked to enter the problem types you want to analyze (for example, 50–50 WIN). The pro-

gram will tell you how problem types will be coded in the third column of your data file.

2. *Dependent variable.* You can include the data from any of the dependent variables in the fourth column of the data file.

3. *Data file information.* You need to specify a path to the folder containing the data files. Simply open any data file and the path will be set.

4. *Output file information.* You can create a custom name for the output file, include participant numbers in the first column, and separate the output columns by spaces or tabs. Including participant numbers allows you to hand-code additional conditions. For example, if participants 1 through 10 were in the E-Sim condition, you could use the participant numbers to code them all with a 1 in the data file.

5. *From . . . To . . .* You can specify a range of participant numbers to analyze. The program will look for participant data files only in the folder specified in the data file path.

6. *Saving and loading your analysis parameters.* Double-clicking an analysis parameter file will automatically reinstate your saved analysis, including data file paths.

Additional analysis help is available in the program. A demonstration of how to use the *Stroop Analysis* software is available in Appendix B. The *JCT Analysis* software will work the same way.

Suggested Projects

☆ 1. You can replicate the original Alloy et al. (1981) experiment. The materials you need are available in Chapter 7. Because you probably will not have a clinically depressed population available, you could look at changing from a nondepressed baseline to either elated or depressed mood. Do participants who start out nondepressed increase or decrease in judged control the same way depressed participants do?

2. You can replicate the experiment in Alloy et al. (1981) but include different groups. Some suggestions:

☆☆ a. Induce mood using a different technique. Pignatiello, Camp, and Rasar (1986) present a musical mood-induction technique as an alternative to the Velten technique used by Alloy et al. (1981). Does a music D-Ind group behave the same way as a Velten D-Ind group? Additional mood-induction techniques are suggested in Chapter 7.

☆☆ b. How would a control group with a simple judgment problem perform? The participants in Alloy et al. (1981) all saw the 50–50 WIN problem. How would participants act if they were merely judging control without winning any money? Alternatively, how would participants act in a 50–50 LOSE problem?

☆☆ c. How much money does it take to get the illusion of control? If participants were playing for a penny a trial, would that change the magnitude of the illusion relative to participants playing for $10 a trial?

☆☆☆ 3. Alloy et al. (1981) demonstrated that changing people's moods will change their perception of control. That does not rule out the possibility that changing people's perceived control will affect their mood. One way you might test this is to gather a group of nondepressed people and induce them to depression. Then, give some of them a 100% control task using Alloy et al.'s procedure and give others a 0% control task. Will participants with 100% control improve from their initially depressed state more than participants with 0% control?

4. You can look at perceived control based on other variables that should affect mood. Some suggestions:

☆☆☆   a. Baum and colleagues (Baum, Aiello, & Calesnick, 1978; Baum and Gatchel, 1981) found that crowding in a college dormitory can lead to feelings of helplessness. The less possible it was for people to avoid unwanted contact, the more helpless they felt. You might investigate the effects of crowding or other environmental factors on perceived control.

☆☆☆   b. McIntosh, Keywell, Reifman, and Ellsworth (1994) found that for women in law school, overall health declined and depression increased relative to men as the school year progressed. It might be possible that this is a function of stress due to lack of control (similar to crowding). As the semester progresses, pressures build. You could assess control at several time slices during the semester to see if judged control changes with changing levels of stress.

☆☆☆   c. Barkley and Tryon (1995) found that depressed participants were less active than nondepressed controls in an unmedicated, outpatient population. This extended a large body of research showing that depression slows motor performance. You can replicate Alloy et al. (1981) using faster settings for the presentation rates. Perhaps D-Ind participants will have more difficulty with fast presentation than E-Ind participants.

■ ■ ■ ■ ■ ■
References

Alloy, L. B., & Abramson, L. Y. (1979). Judgment of contingency in depressed and nondepressed students: Sadder but wiser? *Journal of Experimental Psychology: General, 4,* 441–485. Used with permission of the author.

Alloy, L. B., Abramson, L. Y., & Viscusi, D. (1981). Induced mood and the illusion of control. *Journal of Personality and Social Psychology, 41,* 1129–1140. Used with permission of the author.

Barkley, T. J., & Tryon, W. W. (1995). Psychomotor retardation found in college students seeking counseling. *Behaviour Research and Therapy, 33,* 977–984.

Baum, A., Aiello, J. R., & Calesnick, L. E. (1978). Crowding and personal control: Social density and the development of learned helplessness. *Journal of Personality and Social Psychology, 36,* 1000–1011.

Baum, A., & Gatchel, R. J. (1981). Cognitive determinants of reaction to uncontrollable events: Development of reactance and learned helplessness. *Journal of Personality and Social Psychology, 40,* 1078–1089.

Gatchel, R. J., Paulus, P. B., & Maples, C. W. (1975). Learned helplessness and self-reported affect. *Journal of Abnormal Psychology, 84,* 732–734.

McIntosh, D. N., Keywell, J., Reifman, A., & Ellsworth, P. C. (1994). Stress and health in first-year law students: Women fare worse. *Journal of Applied Social Psychology, 24,* 1474–1499.

Pignatiello, M. F., Camp, C. J., & Rasar, L. A. (1986). Musical mood induction: An alternative to the Velten technique. *Journal of Abnormal Psychology, 95,* 295–297.

Seligman, M. E. P., & Maier, S. F. (1967). Failure to escape traumatic shock. *Journal of Experimental Psychology, 74,* 1–9.

Velten, E. C. (1968). A laboratory task for induction of mood states. *Behaviour Research and Therapy, 6,* 473–482.

Getting Approval from Institutional Review Boards

To ensure that research follows ethical guidelines and to protect participants from harm, research projects must be reviewed by an Institutional Review Board (IRB). This appendix describes the questions that will be asked by the IRB, along with some suggestions for appropriate answers. A completed IRB form has been included at the end of the appendix.

The Questions

The American Psychological Association (1992) has adopted a set of ethical guidelines to protect research participants from harm. It is the responsibility of experimenters to follow these guidelines. You should familiarize yourself with these rules before beginning your project.

Some institutions will allow your instructor to serve as the Institutional Review Board (IRB) that will review your project. Most will require a more formal procedure. This appendix provides some guidelines for completing IRB forms. The simplest way to get approval is to make sure your project follows the ethical principles. There should be no risk to participants, no potential for harm, and minimal or no deception; and the research question itself should have merit.

Some questions follow that you will be asked to complete for the IRB, along with some suggestions for how to answer them. A completed IRB form has been included at the end of this appendix.

Project Description

What is your research question? What will participants do in your experiment? What materials will they see? If a person on the IRB perceives a risk to participants, you will not be allowed to carry on with your project. Your proposal will also be held up if your description is unclear. A sample description is presented

179

below. The title for this proposal was "Marijuana Use and the Generation Effect." The project was conducted by Leigh Anne Dempsey, Marty Hester, and Daniel Brown of Middle Tennessee State University.

> We will first administer a brief survey to participants that asks about prior drug use (attached). After the survey, participants will be asked to memorize two lists of words. For one list, they will generate the words to be remembered by using a cue word and the first letter of the target word (for example, the cue may be "grape," and they generate a word that rhymes with grape and starts with "a"). For the second list, participants will read the words ("grape" and "ape" are both presented together). The two lists will have different words. Previous research has shown that generating words improves memory over reading them, we want to see if the magnitude of this effect is the same for people who have smoked marijuana as for people who have not.

After the IRB reviewed this project, they expressed some concern about confidentiality. One of the ethical rules is that participants' results must be confidential. Because prior drug use is very personal information, the IRB were concerned that there be no way to match a participant's survey to his or her name. This paragraph was added to the project description:

> Each participant will be assigned a number on their survey. That number will be used to match their memory data to their survey responses. The surveys will be deposited in a sealed box after completion. When the study is finished, we will open the box and score the surveys all at once.

With this procedure, there is less chance that the experimenter will know whether or not a particular participant completed a particular survey. In order to compute a correlation between marijuana use and memory, a system had to be devised to match the two pieces of information while maintaining confidentiality. By working with the IRB, the students were able to carry out their project in an ethical manner.

Here is a more straightforward description. (This project was conducted by Tracey Fox, Patti Saulter, and Neil Norman of Middle Tennessee State University; the results appear as the sample poster in Appendix D.)

> Previous research suggests that blue arouses soothed feelings and red arouses tense feelings. However, the effects are generally small, and the results are somewhat inconsistent. We will replicate previous room-color research with a new dependent variable that should be more sensitive to changes in mood, if any occur.
>
> Participants will spend 10 minutes in either a blue room, a red room, or a white room. They will complete Tangram puzzles during this interval. Then, they will complete three conditions of a Stroop interference task. One condition will involve naming the colors of tense words ("tense," "excited," "aroused," "hostile"), one condition will involve naming the colors of soothing words ("relaxed," "serene," "soothed," "peace"), and

one condition will involve neutral words ("one," "two," "three," "four"). There will be eight repetitions of each word in each condition for 48 tense trials, 48 soothed trials, and 48 neutral trials. We expect mood-congruent words to produce more interference. So, for example, red-room participants should take longer for tense words than for soothed words or neutral words when naming the colors.

The Stroop task will be implemented using a Macintosh computer. The room color will be manipulated by placing theatrical lighting gels over lamps in the room to bathe the walls in the appropriate color.

This project was approved on the first submission. The motivation is clear, the task is explained well, and there are no potential risks for participants.

Confidentiality

A special procedural issue is how you plan to keep participants' results confidential. This has two components:

1. How will you ensure anonymity (nobody knows who participated in your study)?
2. How will you keep results confidential?

A little of this was already included in the description above for the marijuana and memory experiment. Some IRBs will ask a question that specifically deals with how you will ensure confidentiality. Here is a sample from a simple experimental procedure in which participants complete the experiment using computers:

> Participants will sign a consent form. These will be kept separate from the data. Their name and any other identifying information will not be recorded anywhere else. The data files produced by the experiment software will not contain identifying information. Participants will complete the experiment in private with other participants using the computers.

Unless you have a special circumstance (like the marijuana experiment above), this type of response will be adequate. None of your materials should ask for participants' names, and there should be no way to match data with names.

Participant Population

Who will participate? Our form at Middle Tennessee State University has check boxes for a variety of populations (adult, minor, prisoner, mentally retarded, mentally ill, physically ill, disabled, and other). If you are using college-age adults who do not fall into any other category, the approval process is simple. Whenever you plan to study a population that may not be able to freely volunteer (e.g., minors or prisoners), there will be extra steps to the permission process. For example, if you want to study children, you will have to explain how they will be contacted, how you will get parental consent, and how you will get consent from your participants. You will also need permission from any institution involved in the data-collection process. In other words, if you plan to contact children through their schools, you will need permission from the schools. Your institution may have additional rules.

The best population to study in Research Methods Laboratory projects is adults. College students usually form the population. My students frequently include this statement for their population:

> Adult friends of the experimenters will be asked to volunteer to participate.

If you will have a more elaborate sign-up procedure, most IRBs want to know about it. Here is a sample of a sign-up procedure:

> Participants will sign up on the Psychology Department research participant bulletin board. A copy of the sign-up sheet is attached.

Generally speaking, you will not be allowed to go door-to-door looking for participants. The less intrusive your contact method, the better.

Consent

How will participants give their consent to participate? There are several things a consent form should include. First, describe the research. You need to include enough information for a person to make an informed decision about whether or not to participate. If there are special risks or if you are asking for sensitive information, make that very clear. Second, let participants know their rights. The main right is their ability to quit the experiment at any time without penalty. They also have the right to ask questions. Finally, make it clear that the results will be confidential. Most IRBs will want to see a sample of your consent form. Here is one:

CONSENT FORM

PLEASE READ CAREFULLY BEFORE SIGNING.
I have agreed to participate in the experiment, "The effect of orientational metaphors on text comprehension," and hereby give my consent to be a participant. I understand that I will read 31 texts from a computer monitor and answer questions after each text. The experiment will take approximately 45 minutes to complete. I understand that there are no risks for me as a participant. I have the right to ask questions about what I will be expected to do in the experiment. I understand that my responses will be kept in the strictest of confidence and anonymity. I have the option to withdraw from the experiment at any time with no penalty or loss of credit. I understand that the experiment will be explained to me after my participation is complete, and I may ask questions at that time.

Debriefing

You are required to provide a full explanation of the experiment after participants are finished. This is usually a verbal description. It is also nice to give participants a sheet with a simple description and a phone number they can call
with questions or to find out the results of the experiment. Here is a sample
debriefing sheet:

> In this experiment we were investigating ways to improve people's
> comprehension of complicated texts. Previous research has shown that
> pictures help. We were interested in finding out if your prior knowledge
> about the way the world works would also help. All of the text arrange-
> ments had this basic shape:

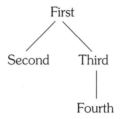

> To answer the questions based on the text, it was necessary to know this
> shape. To help get the shape, some of the people were instructed to think
> of MORE as UP. We were hoping that this mapping onto a spatial
> dimension would improve their ability to understand the texts. Others saw
> a picture of the arrangement, and others received no help at all. If you
> would like to know the results or have further questions, feel free to
> contact Dr. Langston at ####. Thanks for your participation.

Special Information

Some projects will require more information. Any project involving deception,
special participant populations, or risk to participants will have to be justified.
You will be required to explain why successful completion of the project requires these elements. You will have to explain how the potential harm to participants is offset by the value of the knowledge to be gained. You will also have
to explain how you have tried to minimize harm, even in these situations, and
why other ways of conducting the research will not work.

As a rule of thumb, avoid the use of deception. It has the potential to harm
participants, and it can make participants suspicious of research (for more on
both of these issues, I suggest reading Epley & Huff, 1998). For your research
methods lab projects, there will almost always be another way to carry out your
experiment that does not involve deception.

■ ■ ■ ■ ■ ■
A Completed Form

This is an exact copy of an IRB form completed by a group of students in one of my classes. All of their answers have been included. Note that your institution's form will be slightly different from this form.

PLEASE PRINT OR TYPE	PROTOCOL NUMBER: SUBMISSION DATE:

MIDDLE TENNESSEE STATE UNIVERSITY
INSTITUTIONAL REVIEW BOARD
HUMAN SUBJECTS RESEARCH REVIEW FORM

☒ Expedited Review   ☐ Full Review

Investigator(s)' Name(s), SS#(s)   Brian Lee, Carol Paschall, Heather Whitehead, and Troy Vaughn (social security numbers have been deleted)

Project Title   Can People Detect the Meaning of Reversed Speech?

Campus telephone   ###-####

Campus address   MTSU Box ###

Department or University Unit   Psychology

Investigator Status (For each investigator):

☐ Faculty/Staff
☐ Graduate Student
☒ Undergraduate Student
☐ Other

If the principle investigator is a student, list name, department, and local telephone of faculty supervisor. Please note that THE FACULTY SUPERVISOR MUST INDICATE KNOWLEDGE AND APPROVAL OF THIS PROPOSAL BY SIGNING THIS FORM.

Faculty Supervisor Name   William Langston

Address & Telephone   MTSU Box ###, ####

Source of funding for project   None

Expected starting date for project   March 29, 1999

Is this project expected to continue for more than one year?

☐ Yes   ☒ No   Anticipated Completion Date   April 15, 1999

Form copyright © MTSU Office of Sponsored Programs, used by permission. The students' responses are also used by permission.

PROJECT DESCRIPTION

- The following information is required for all projects.
- Limit your answers to the space provided. (Further information may be attached to supplement this description, but not to replace it.)
- Attach copies of all questionnaires, testing instruments, or interview protocols; include any cover letters or instructions to subject.

DESCRIPTION

Provide a **BRIEF** description, in **LAYPERSON'S TERMS**, of the proposed research:

Some people claim that when people lie, they tell the truth in reverse. This hypothesis flies in the face of current research on speech production. We want to test the reverse speech hypothesis (elucidated most clearly at www.reversespeech.com). Our reasoning is that if these messages are being sent, then people ought to be able to receive them. This reception may be unconscious (as in a vague feeling that a person is not being truthful). A lot of research shows that people have increased arousal to physical threat words. Will people show this arousal if the words are played in reverse speech? We will play a sample of neutral words and a sample of physical threat words both forwards and backwards (word lists attached). Participants will then rate their anxiety using a likert-type scale (attached). If participants can unconsciously interpret the feeling conveyed by reverse speech, we should see equivalent arousal in the forwards and backwards groups. If we don't see arousal in the backwards group, that would suggest that people cannot detect the meaning of reversed speech.

METHOD (check all that apply)

- ☐ QUESTIONNAIRE   ☐ OBSERVATION   ☐ TEST
- ☐ INTERVIEW   ☐ FILES   ☒ TASK
- ☐ TREATMENT
- ☐ OTHER _____

NUMBER OF SUBJECTS

60

SUBJECT POPULATION (check all that apply)

- ☒ ADULT   ☐ MINOR
- ☐ PRISONER   ☐ MENTALLY RETARDED
- ☐ MENTALLY ILL   ☐ PHYSICALLY ILL
- ☐ DISABLED   ☐ OTHER
  Specify: _____

SUBJECT SELECTION

Are subjects to be drawn from the Psychology subject pool? (Y/N)   <u>N</u>

- If yes, a completed sample sign-up sheet must be submitted.
- If no, describe how subjects will be selected for participation in this project and any payment to be received by the subject:

Adult friends of the experimenters will be asked to volunteer to participate.

NOTE: If the subjects are to be drawn from an institution or organization (e.g. hospital, social service agency, prison, school, etc.) which has the responsibility for the subjects, then documentation of permission from that institution must be submitted to the Board before final approval can be given.

CONFIDENTIALITY

Specify steps to be taken to guard the anonymity of subjects and/or the confidentiality of their responses. Indicate what personal identifying indicators will be kept on subjects. Specify procedures for storage and ultimate disposal of personal information.

No identifying information will be collected. Consent forms will be kept separate from the data.

CONSENT

Specify how subjects will be informed of the following: (a) the nature of their participation in the project, (b) that their participation is voluntary and that they may withdraw at any time without repercussions, and (c) that their responses are confidential. (If a consent form is being used, attach a copy. If presented orally, a copy of the presentation must be submitted.)

CONSENT FORM
PLEASE READ CAREFULLY BEFORE SIGNING

I have agreed to participate in the experiment "Can People Detect the Meaning of Reversed Speech?" and hereby give my consent to be a participant. I understand that I will listen to approximately 12 minutes of words and complete a brief questionnaire. I may find some of the words to be offensive or unpleasant. I may stop at any time if I feel uncomfortable. The experiment will take approximately 20 minutes to complete. I have the right to ask questions about what I will be expected to do in the experiment. I understand that my responses will be kept in the strictest of confidence and anonymity. I have the option to withdraw from the experiment at any time with no penalty or loss of credit earned at that time. I understand that the experiment will be explained to me after my participation is complete, and I may ask questions at that time. If I have any additional questions I may call Dr. William Langston at ###-####.

_____
Participant's name   (Please Print)

_____   _____
Participant's signature   Investigator's signature

_____   _____
Date   Date

ADDITIONAL PROCEDURAL INFORMATION

INDICATE BELOW WHETHER YOUR PROJECT INVOLVES ANY OF THE FOLLOWING. FOR EACH ITEM CHECKED, PROVIDE THE REQUESTED INFORMATION IN THE ADDITIONAL PROCEDURAL INFORMATION SECTION BEGINNING ON PAGE 5.

☐ A) Risk (p. 5)
☐ B) Minors as subjects (p. 5)
☐ C) Psychological intervention (p. 6)
☐ D) Deception (p. 6)
☐ E) Physiological intervention (p. 7)
☐ F) Biomedical procedures (p. 7)

> **SEE THE PAGE INDICATED FOR A MORE DETAILED DESCRIPTION OF THESE CATEGORIES**

SIGNATURES

The **Principal Investigator** must sign this form.

> I certify that a) the information provided for this project is accurate, b) no other procedures will be used in this project, and c) any modifications in this project will be submitted for approval prior to use.

_____   _____
Signature of Investigator   **Date**

If the P.I. is a student, his/her **Faculty Supervisor** must also sign this form.

> I certify that this project is under my direct supervision and that I am responsible for insuring that all provisions of approval are complied with by the investigator.

_____   _____
Signature of Faculty Supervisor   **Date**

Committee Use Only

NOTE: APPROVAL OF THIS PROJECT BY THE IRB ONLY SIGNIFIES THAT THE PROCEDURES ADEQUATELY PROTECT THE RIGHTS AND WELFARE OF THE SUBJECTS AND SHOULD NOT BE TAKEN TO INDICATE UNIVERSITY APPROVAL TO CONDUCT THE RESEARCH.

Expedited Review

Approved: _____   _____
                    College Representative   Date

Committee Review

Approved: _____   _____
                    Committee Chair   Date

■ ■ ■ ■ ■ ■
References

American Psychological Association. (1992). Ethical principles of psychologists and code of conduct. *American Psychologist, 47,* 1597–1611.

Epley, N., & Huff, C. (1998). Suspicion, affective response, and educational benefit as a result of deception in psychology research. *Personality and Social Psychology Bulletin, 24,* 759–768.

Using the Analysis Software

The purpose of this appendix is to explain how to operate the analysis software that accompanies the experimental software for Chapters 4, 7, 8, and 11. The exercises in this appendix will take you step by step through an analysis of data collected using the *Stroop Task* software. The same basic procedure can be followed for the other analysis software, and the procedure will be the same for analyzing custom experiments as it is for analyzing an experiment for which parameters have been provided.

■ ■ ■ ■ ■ ■
Step 1: Organize the Data

The first step is to organize the data. Gather all of the data files into a single folder. All of the participants you include in the analysis should have been run using the same parameter settings. For high internal validity, you should never mix data from participants in different experiments. All of the files should end in "P#." The "#" is a participant number and should be unique for each participant. Ideally, this will be the same number that you used when you collected the data. You can change the names of the data files to anything you want as long as they end in P#. It is much simpler if you use the generic file names. For the Stroop task, the generic names are "StroopP#."

■ ■ ■ ■ ■ ■
Step 2: Look at the Data

Once the data are prepared, you can begin the analysis. Sample Stroop data files are in the folder "Sample Stroop Data." These data were provided by students in my research methods class in the summer of 1999. There are 20 data files in the folder, numbered from 1 to 20. The raw files are in a format that would not make any sense if you tried to read it. To prepare the files for viewing, you need to process them with the analysis program.

You can view the contents of any one of the data files by double-clicking it. This launches the *Stroop Analysis* program and puts you into the output utility. Click "Output," and the data will be output to a file called "Participant Data."

If the program is already running, you can choose "Output Data File" from the main screen of the *Stroop Analysis* program (Macintosh users will choose "Print Data" from the "Analysis Menu"). You will have to choose a file to view and specify a location to save the data. (Macintosh users can also print directly to the printer, but that option is a little shaky.) Once the program is running, double-clicking a file will no longer work. You should choose files to view from within the program.

I suggest that you look at a few of the sample data files so that you know how the data are stored. This step can help with the analysis that we will do next. Condition 1 in this experiment was color words written in mismatching colors. Condition 2 was colored boxes.

■■■■■■
Step 3: Begin an Analysis

Now that you have had a chance to look at some data, let's perform an analysis. Double-click the *Stroop Analysis* program icon if the program is not already running. Choose "Analyze Data" from the main screen (Macintosh users will choose "Analyze Data" from the "Analysis Menu"). You will get the analysis screen in Figure B.1.

Figure B.1 *Stroop Analysis* analysis screen.

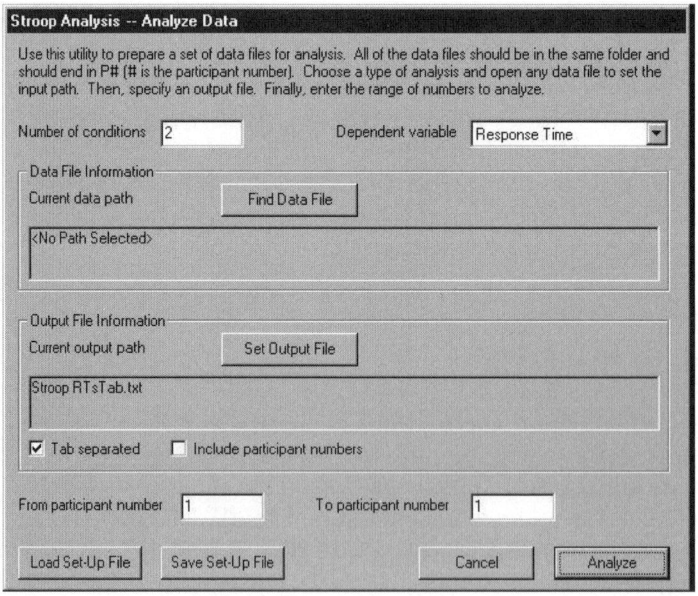

Setting up an analysis is very simple. First, enter the number of conditions. My sample experiment had two conditions. Then, choose a dependent variable. We will start by looking at response times, which is the default setting.

The next step is to open any data file in the data folder. This will set a path that the program will use to open all of the files. A default name will be provided for the output file. This name is "Stroop" plus a description of the file's contents. If you analyze response times, then "RTs" will be appended to the name. If you analyze accuracy, then "Acc" will be appended to the name. The data in your output file can be separated by spaces or tabs. Most statistics packages will prefer that the data be separated by tabs. If your file will be separated by spaces, the file name will end in "Spc." If your file will be separated by tabs, the name will end in "Tab." Click "Set Output File" and choose a location to save the results of the analysis (for the Macintosh version, the default path will be to the folder with the data).

Check "Include participant numbers" to include the participant numbers in the file. Participant numbers, if they are included, will be the first column. Participant numbers are useful because they allow you to match up data from different analyses. Note that the number included in the analysis is the number you entered when you collected the data. If you change the name of a file on the desktop, the number reported with the analysis will be whatever is stored in the data file, not the number in the file name.

The last step is to put "20" in the "To Participant Number" box. The analysis is ready to run. Figure B.2 shows what my screen looks like at this point.

Click "Analyze" to analyze the data.

Figure B.2 *Stroop Analysis* analysis screen, ready to analyze the sample data.

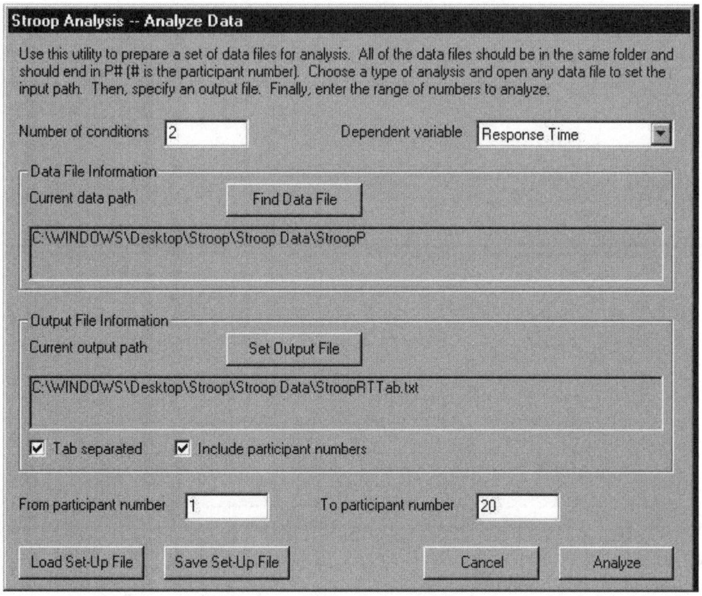

■ ■ ■ ■ ■ ■
Step 4: Check the Data

Double-click the file that you just created, and you can see the results of the analysis. The contents of my file are presented in Table B.1. The first column contains participant numbers, the second column contains the average response times for condition 1 (color words), and the third column contains the average response times for condition 2 (colored boxes). Note that Windows users will see the times in seconds (as they are here). The Macintosh version reports times in ms (1 ms = 1/1000 of a second).

The first thing you may notice is that two of the participants (numbers 2 and 11) have zero in the first condition. In other words, there were no times recorded for those two participants for condition 1. Condition 1 is the color word condition. Perhaps the task was so hard for these participants that they

Table B.1 Response Time Data for the Sample Stroop Data Files*

1	1.33	0.62
2	0	1.16
3	1.22	0.7
4	1.26	0.95
5	1.02	0.72
6	1.08	0.8
7	0.93	1.98
8	0.93	0.69
9	0.7	0.57
10	1.37	0.96
11	0	0.53
12	0.66	0.78
13	1.04	0.73
14	0.69	0.53
15	1.1	1.35
16	0.97	0.62
17	1.28	0.76
18	0.57	0.47
19	1	0.95
20	1.21	0.66

*The first column contains participant numbers, the second column contains times from condition 1, and the third column contains times from condition 2.

could not answer any of the trials correctly. A more likely explanation is that the participants misunderstood the instructions. Instead of naming the color, they responded with the word. How can you tell if that is really what happened? At this point, you cannot; but, if you debrief your participants correctly, they will tell you after the experiment what they did, and you can note their numbers for future reference. I know from collecting the data that three participants misunderstood the instructions. The two with zeros are obvious. The third person figured out her error part way through the experiment, so she answered at least some trials correctly. I think all of these participants should be excluded from the analysis. We are interested in regular responding, not responses from people who misunderstood the instructions. How can we find the third person? There should be a lot of errors. Let's look at an analysis of percent correct. Figure B.3 shows the screen after it is set up for that analysis.

Figure B.3 *Stroop Analysis* analysis screen, ready to analyze percent correct.

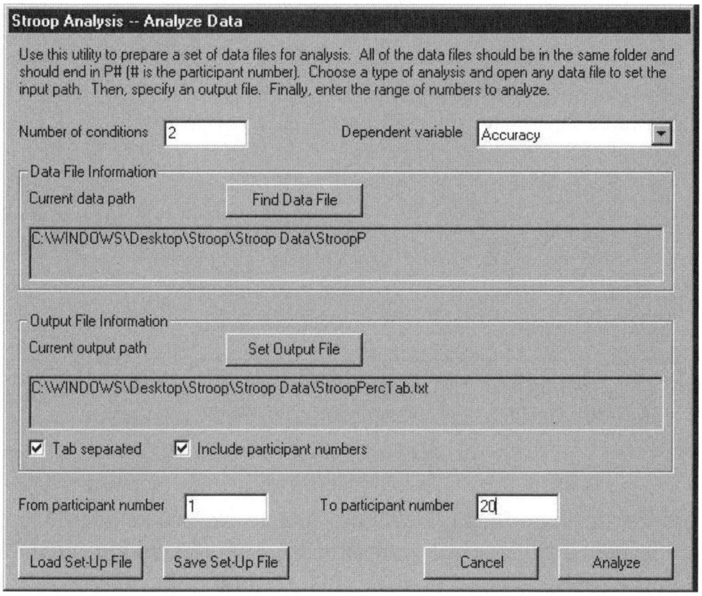

The only difference from before is that I have chosen "Accuracy" from the dependent variable menu. The data for percent correct are presented in Table B.2.

This is where participant numbers can really help. Participants 2 and 11 had zero for their times. They also have 0% correct. A quick scan shows me that participant 1 is the other person whose data I want to exclude. She had 2% correct for the color words.

What we have been doing so far is checking the data. It is always a good idea to look through your data to see if everything looks correct. In this case, even if we had not taken careful notes when running the experiment, we could

Table B.2 Percent Correct Data for the Sample Stroop Data Files*

1	2	100
2	0	98
3	96	94
4	98	100
5	98	100
6	98	94
7	100	96
8	92	98
9	100	100
10	98	98
11	0	96
12	100	100
13	98	100
14	98	98
15	84	76
16	98	98
17	98	92
18	96	100
19	98	100
20	100	100

*The first column contains participant numbers, the second column contains percents from condition 1, and the third column contains percents from condition 2.

still find the three participants whose data should be excluded. I know from the data collection that one other participant's data should also be excluded. Look through the reaction times and see if you can spot her data.

The person to exclude is participant 7. However, if you did not already know that, you would be faced with a real dilemma right now. The Stroop effect is that the times for naming the colors of color words will be longer than for naming the colors of colored boxes. Participant 7 took 0.93 sec for color words and 1.98 sec for colored boxes. This is a pretty striking reversal of the Stroop effect. In fact, I can tell you that, with her data included, the effect is not significant. So, we would like to exclude her; but we cannot just throw out every participant who does not fit the expected pattern. If you do not take careful notes during the experiment, and if you do not carefully debrief your participants, you will not be able to exclude participants with data like these. You are right to suspect that something unusual occurred, but if you do not know for sure, you have to leave her in. However, I know that this participant thought her computer was locked

Table B.3 Response Time Data for the Sample Stroop
Data Files After Removing Invalid Data*

3	1.22	0.7
4	1.26	0.95
5	1.02	0.72
6	1.08	0.8
8	0.93	0.69
9	0.7	0.57
10	1.37	0.96
12	0.66	0.78
13	1.04	0.73
14	0.69	0.53
15	1.1	1.35
16	0.97	0.62
17	1.28	0.76
18	0.57	0.47
19	1	0.95
20	1.21	0.66

*The first column contains participant numbers, the
second column contains times from condition one, and
the third column contains times from condition 2.

up. She came to get me from the waiting room where I was organizing the next group of participants. By the time we got back and found out that the computer was working, a five-minute reaction time had been recorded. That one time has skewed her results. So, we can take her out of the analysis. My reaction time data after checking are presented in Table B.3.

I have removed the data for participants 1, 2, 7, and 11. It is unusual to exclude 20% of the data. What this suggests is that the experimenter did not explain the procedure carefully enough. Fortunately, careful note taking during the experiment overcame my poor explanation of the procedure.

You can learn a couple of lessons from this. First, collecting data from people is not the same as getting responses from a machine. People will sometimes misunderstand or do strange things. A good experimenter will prevent as many mistakes as possible and be aware of any that were not prevented. Taking the time to talk to your participants really helps with the data collection. The second lesson is that you should always check your data. If you have a lot of strange data in your results, you can recognize problems that a statistical analysis cannot pick up. For example, no analysis program would have pointed out the problem with participant 7. The analysis program analyzes whatever you give it, even if what you give it is corrupted in some way.

■ ■ ■ ■ ■ ■
Step 5: Import the Data into a Statistics Package

Now that you have analyzed the results and checked them, it is time to open your statistics package. The specific program you use will determine how to import the data. Usually, if you separate the columns with tabs ("tab-delimited"), import will be no problem.

To be sure you have set up the analysis correctly, my results from the *t*-test on the response time data (from SPSS) are presented in Table B.4.

Table B.4 Response Time *t*-test Results for the Sample Stroop Data Files (from SPSS)

Variable	Number of Pairs	Corr	2-tail Sig	Mean	SD	SE of Mean
VAR1				1.0069	.242	.060
	16	.524	.037			
VAR2				.7639	.213	.053

Paired Differences					
Mean	SD	SE of Mean	t-value	df	2-tail Sig
.2429	.223	.056	4.35	15	.001

The first part provides descriptive statistics. The color word mean was 1.01 seconds (*SD* = 0.24), and the colored box mean was 0.76 seconds (*SD* = 0.21). Is this difference significant? If you look at the *t*-value, you see that it is 4.35. The "2-tail Sig" (or *p*) is .001. Because this is less than .05, the difference between the means is significant.

Now, is there a difference in percent correct? Import the accuracy data and compute the *t* test. My results are presented in Table B.5. You should find the same outcome.

As you can see, the *t* test for accuracy is not significant. Overall, the participants were very accurate (approximately 97% in both conditions).

Table B.5 Percent Correct *t*-test Results for the Sample Stroop Data Files (from SPSS)

Variable	Number of Pairs	Corr	2-tail Sig	Mean	SD	SE of Mean
VAR1				.9688	.039	.010
	16	.838	.000			
VAR2				.9675	.061	.015

Paired Differences					
Mean	SD	SE of Mean	t-value	df	2-tail Sig
.0013	.035	.009	.14	15	.889

■ ■ ■ ■ ■ ■
Step 6: Interpret and Report

You have completed the analysis; but you are not finished with your project yet. What do the results mean? How should you report these results in your paper? Which results should you report? For more on this topic, turn to Appendix C. That appendix covers writing results sections.

Writing Results Sections

This appendix describes how to write a results section. The process is described from choosing the appropriate statistic to deciding how much information to include in the report. For information on preparing the rest of the manuscript, I suggest that you consult Rosnow and Rosnow (2001). Their brief introduction to APA style focuses on the information a student would need to prepare a paper. It also includes sample research reports.

Choosing a Statistic

Figure C.1 contains a decision tree that you can use to choose the appropriate statistic for your design. To use the tree, you will answer a series of questions about your design. You will start by deciding what type of statistical question you are trying to answer. You can answer questions about differences between means, frequencies, or relationships. If you are unsure of the kind of question you have, the following guidelines might be useful (however, they are only general guidelines, violations of them are common). Experiments will generally involve questions about differences between means. Observation designs will generally involve questions about frequencies. Correlation and survey designs will generally involve questions about relationships. Once you know what kind of question you are asking, you will make decisions based on the specific design you used.

As an example, let's say I ran a simple version of Stroop's Experiment 2. I had 20 participants name the colors of colored words and the colors of colored boxes. I want to know if the naming time for words differs from the naming time for boxes.

At the first node, I choose the "differences between means" branch. That is because I want to know if the two mean naming times differ from one another. I have two conditions (words and boxes), so I choose "Two conditions." Because the same people were in each group, that is the next branch I take (for

Figure C.1 A statistical decision tree.

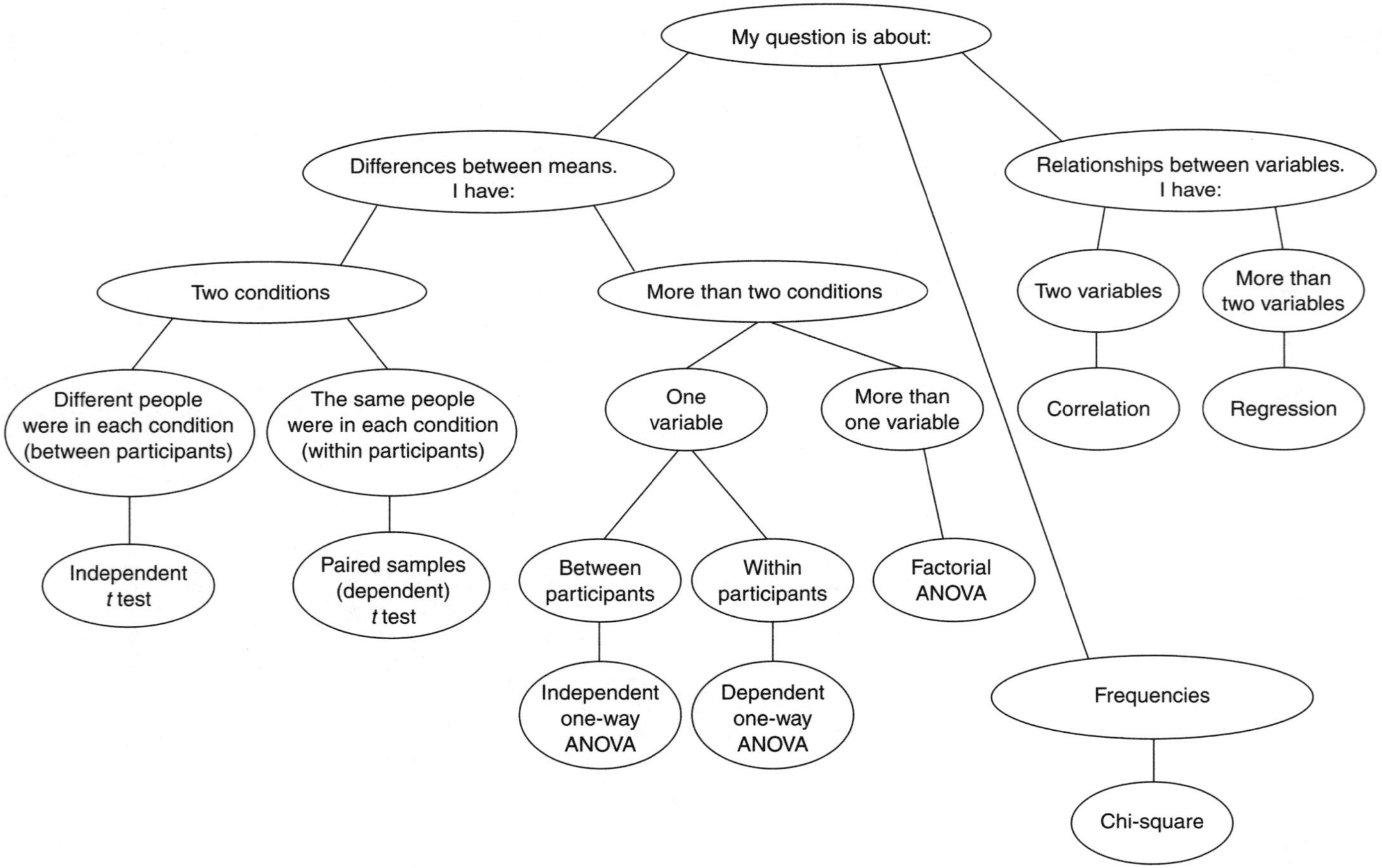

within participants). That leads me to a "paired samples *t* test." So, the appropriate statistic for this design is a paired samples *t* test.

At this point, with the statistic chosen, it is time to perform some computations. You can do this by hand, using your notes from statistics, or you can use a statistics software package. Once that is done, you are ready to write.

■ ■ ■ ■ ■ ■
What to Say?

Each statistic will require a slightly different write-up. The general rule is to include enough information for the person reading your paper to understand your computations. Included here are sample results sections for each of the main statistics. (For all of these, I consulted Glenberg [1996] to help determine what to report. Some of the results sections below use his formatting. His text is an excellent source for additional information on statistics.)

Chi-square

A chi-square test can be used to find out if two frequency distributions are independent of one another. These tests are often conducted after observation designs in which frequency data are collected. For example, let's say I went to the library to observe the territorial markers that people use. I want to know if the type of marker used is independent of the gender of the person placing the marker. Loosely speaking, do men and women use the same types of territorial markers? I decide to observe three marker types: placing a book bag or similar item on an adjacent chair, spreading out materials on the table top, or rearranging the furniture to create more personal space. I chose these three markers based on a literature review. I went to the library and observed the first 30 men and the first 30 women to sit at a specified table. I classified them based on the first of the three markers that they used. My data are presented in Table C.1.

Table C.1 Frequency of Using a Territorial Marker as a Function of Gender

	Gender	
Marker	Women	Men
Bag in chair (*n* = 17)	8	9
Papers spread out (*n* = 23)	16	7
Move furniture (*n* = 20)	6	14
Total	30	30

A quick glance at the frequencies suggests that the two distributions (men and women) are not independent. In other words, the frequency of using a particular marker seems to depend on gender. The chi-square test of independence can tell me if that is the case. After computing the chi-square, I find that there is enough evidence to conclude that the two distributions are not independent. The value for the chi-square is 6.78, $p < .05$. Here is the results section reporting that:

> The territorial marker frequency distributions for men and women were compared using a chi-square test of independence. The frequencies are presented in Table C.1. The chi-square was significant, $\chi^2(2, N = 60) = 6.78$, $p < .05$. Men were more likely to move furniture than women, women were more likely to spread papers than men.

Correlation

A correlation is computed when you want to assess the strength and direction of the relationship between two measured variables. The main thing to report is the correlation itself.

For the results section below, two students observed men as they selected pornographic videos. They recorded the time to make a selection and the number of men who intruded while a man was selecting a video. The students were interested in the relationship between the number of intruders and time to choose a video. Based on other research on territoriality, they expected a positive relationship (the more intruders the longer it takes). Here is a results section reporting the correlation:

> Video selection times ranged from 0.2 min to 55.4 min ($M = 11.9$ min, $SD = 9.8$). The number of intruders ranged from 0.0 intruders to 8.0 intruders ($M = 0.8$ intruders, $SD = 1.2$). There was a significant, positive correlation between the number of intruders and time to choose a pornographic video, $r = .59$, $p < .01$. The more intruders there were, the longer men took to choose a video.

t test

A *t* test is used when you want to compare the means of two conditions. If the same people are in both conditions, you will use a dependent *t* test. If different people are in the two conditions, you will use an independent *t* test. You need to report the descriptive statistics for the two conditions and the value of the *t* statistic.

For the sample results section, we will use the simple Stroop experiment described in Appendix B. Participants named the colors of 50 colored boxes and 50 color words. The same people did both tasks. I want to know if the means are different. The results from the experiment (from SPSS) are presented in Table C.2.

Table C.2 Response Time *t*-test Results for the Stroop Experiment (from SPSS)

Variable	Number of Pairs	Corr	2-tail Sig	Mean	SD	SE of Mean
VAR1				1.0069	.242	.060
	16	.524	.037			
VAR2				.7639	.213	.053

Paired Differences					
Mean	SD	SE of Mean	t-value	df	2-tail Sig
.2429	.223	.056	4.35	15	.001

Here is an example of how to report these results:

The data were analyzed using a dependent samples *t* test. The independent variable was the form in which the colors were presented, and the conditions were color words and colored boxes. The dependent variable was reaction time in seconds. The mean reaction times for color words and colored boxes were 1.01 s (*SD* = .24) and 0.76 s (*SD* = .21) respectively. With alpha = .05, the two population means were significantly different, *t*(15) = 4.35, *p* = .001. (Report format from Glenberg, 1996)

ANOVA

■ One-way

This analysis is used when you have one independent variable with more than two conditions. You will need to report whether or not there was a significant difference for the independent variable. You can tell if there is a significant difference by looking under *p* (or probability or significance) in your ANOVA source table.

Imagine that we have carried out the following experiment. We want to know if mood influences perception. We place participants in a sad, neutral, or happy mood using the Velten procedure described in Chapter 7. Participants then read a story and write an ending for it. We count the number of sad words in their story endings. People in sad moods are expected to include more sad words in their stories than people in neutral and happy moods. A source table from that experiment (a modified version of a source table from SPSS) is presented in Table C.3.

Table C.3 ANOVA Source Table for the Mood Experiment

Source of Variation	Sum of Squares	DF	Mean Square	F	Sig of F
MOOD	40.200	2	20.100	24.120	.000
Error	22.500	27	.833		

Table C.4 Number of Sad Words in Story Endings as a Function of Mood

Mood	M	SD
Sad	4.7	0.8
Neutral	2.6	1.1
Happy	2.0	0.8

The descriptive statistics for the experiment are presented in Table C.4.

The *p* value for mood ("Sig of F") is less than .05, so the effect is significant. All I know so far is that within all possible pairwise comparisons of moods (sad vs. neutral, sad vs. happy, and neutral vs. happy), at least one pair is significantly different. I can find out which pairs differ by conducting pairwise comparisons (also called post hoc tests). Any time you have more than two conditions of the independent variable, you have to carry out pairwise comparisons to find out which conditions really differed from one another. To find the exact procedures for this type of test, you should consult a statistics textbook. For example, Glenberg (1996) describes the procedure for conducting a protected *t* test, the statistic I will report below.

We are now ready to write the results section. As usual, we begin with a description of the analysis, then include all of the statistical information:

> The data were analyzed using a one-way, between-participants ANOVA. The mean for sad mood was 4.7 sad words (*SD* = 0.8), the mean for neutral mood was 2.6 sad words (*SD* = 1.1), and the mean for happy mood was 2.0 sad words (*SD* = 0.8). With alpha = .05, the means were significantly different, $F(2,27) = 24.12$, *MSE* = 0.83, $p < .05$. Protected *t* test comparisons indicated that the differences between sad and neutral and sad and happy were significant. The difference between neutral and happy was not significant.

With the information provided in the results section, your readers could reconstruct the entire source table. That might be necessary if they wanted to compute post hoc comparisons with a different procedure. For example, a reader who preferred to use a more conservative test than the protected *t* procedure reported above could use the numbers you have reported to compute his or her own analysis.

■ Factorial

This analysis is used when you have more than one independent variable. You need to report all of the main effects (the effects of each independent variable) plus any post hoc comparisons for those main effects. You also need to report any interactions (combined effects of two or more independent variables).

Factorial ANOVAs can become very complicated, so you should start with a description of the analysis. First list the factors (independent variables), then the dependent variable, then your α. An example of an opening paragraph is presented below. The experiment involved a mood manipulation with sad and neutral moods. I also manipulated the color of the room to see what effect that had on perception. My three room colors were black, peach, and off-white (I could easily obtain access to rooms in these colors). I measured the number of sad words in a story continuation.

The data were analyzed using a two-way between-participants ANOVA. The factors were mood (sad, neutral) and room color (black, peach, off-white). The dependent measure was the number of sad words in a story continuation. For all analyses, the significance level was set at .05.

The next step is to report main effects. For that, you need to consult a source table. The source table for my experiment (a modified version of a source table from SPSS) is presented in Table C.5.

Table C.5 ANOVA Source Table for the Mood and Room Color Experiment

Source of Variation	Sum of Squares	DF	Mean Square	F	Sig of F
Main Effects					
MOOD	16.667	1	16.667	4.839	.041
COLOR	121.333	2	60.667	17.613	.000
2-Way Interactions					
MOOD × COLOR	33.333	2	16.667	4.839	.021
Error	62.000	18	3.444		

The table of means from this design is presented in Table C.6.

Table C.6 Number of Sad Words in Story Endings as a Function of Mood and Room Color

Room Color	Sad		Neutral	
	M	*SD*	*M*	*SD*
Black	10.0	1.6	5.0	1.8
Peach	5.0	2.3	5.0	1.8
Off-white	2.0	0.8	2.0	2.3

The best way to report main effects is to discuss them with respect to a prediction. For example, I predicted that people would write more sad words in a sad mood than in a happy mood. To make the results clear, I will discuss them with this prediction.

If the mood hypothesis were correct, then we would expect a main effect for mood. In particular, the number of sad words in the story continuations should be lower in a neutral mood than in a sad mood. This main effect was significant, $F(1,18) = 4.84$, $MSE = 3.44$, $p < .05$. The means for sad mood and neutral mood were 5.6 sad words ($SD = 3.8$) and 4.0 sad words ($SD = 2.3$), respectively.

Now, I repeat that same paragraph format for the second main effect.

Recall that I also predicted a main effect for room color. In particular, the number of sad words in the story endings should be higher in a black room than in a peach room or an off-white room. This main effect was significant, $F(2,18) = 17.61$, $MSE = 3.44$, $p < .05$. The means for black, peach, and off-white were 7.5 sad words ($SD = 3.1$), 5.0 sad words ($SD = 1.9$), and 2.0 sad words ($SD = 1.6$), respectively. Protected t test comparisons indicated that the differences between all three pairs of means were significant.

The last step is to describe the interaction. First, report whether or not it was significant. Then, choose what will be the "main" independent variable. Describe the differences in the levels of the main independent variable for each level of the other independent variable. One way to do this is to prepare a graph of the data. Once you have the graph, verbally describe it line by line. The means from this experiment are graphed in Figure C.2.

I have chosen mood as the main independent variable and have placed it on the *x* axis. To describe the interaction, I start with the first level of room color and describe the difference between the moods at that level. For example, in a black room, people wrote more sad words in a sad mood than a neutral mood. I would continue in this way until all three lines are described. Here is an example paragraph for the interaction in the experiment described above.

Figure C.2   A graph of the means for the room color and mood experiment.

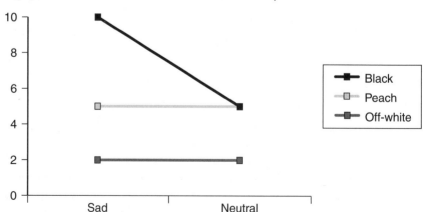

The mood × room color interaction was significant, $F(2,18) = 4.84$, $MSE = 3.44$, $p < .05$. The means are presented in Table C.6. In a black room, fewer sad words were written in a neutral mood than in a sad mood. There was no effect of mood on the number of sad words written in a peach or off-white room.

Note that I cleaned up the description a bit from the procedure described above. Because the effect of mood was the same in both the peach and off-white rooms, I described them together.

If the design had had more independent variables, then there would have been more main effects and interactions. Simply repeat the steps above until everything has been reported. If an effect is not significant, or if you have no prediction about an effect, you may save it until you have discussed all of the important effects. As a general rule, if an effect is significant, you need to report it, even if you had no prediction. If an effect is not significant, you might still want to report the statistical information. Your audience may want to conduct additional analyses that require all of the information from your source table.

Multiple Statistics

Sometimes you will need to report the results of several statistical analyses in one results section. In this case, organization is essential. Try to arrange the results around questions or hypotheses. You may even include headings to identify how one portion of the results section relates to a particular hypothesis. Some additional data from the pornography study described in the correlation section above are presented in Table C.7.

Here is an example of a results section that combines a report of a correlation with a factorial ANOVA (a continuation of the results section reported in the correlation section above):

Video selection times ranged from 0.2 min to 55.4 min ($M = 11.9$ min, $SD = 9.8$). The number of intruders ranged from 0.0 intruders to 8.0 intruders ($M = 0.8$ intruders, $SD = 1.2$). There was a significant positive correlation between the number of intruders and time to choose a pornographic video, $r = .59$, $p < .01$. The more intruders there were, the longer men took to choose a video.

Table C.7 Mean Video Selection Times in Minutes for Main Actors and Intruders as a Function of Intrusion

Actor Type	Intruded Upon			Not Intruded Upon		
	M	*SD*	*n*	*M*	*SD*	*n*
Main actor	19.0	12.6	23	10.5	10.6	20
Intruder	11.6	7.6	26	7.5	4.3	29

The video selection times were compared using a factorial ANOVA. The factors were actor type (main or intruder) and intruded status (intruded upon, not intruded upon). The significance level was set at .05 for all comparisons.

We expected a main effect for actor type. Main actors should take longer than intruders, since intruders should always leave first. In the analysis, there was a main effect for actor type, $F(1,94) = 8.14$, $MSE = 80.7$, $p < .05$. Main actors took longer to select a video (15.1 min, $SD = 12.3$) than did intruders (9.4 min, $SD = 6.4$).

We also expected a main effect for intruded status. Men intruded upon should take longer than men not intruded upon. There was a main effect for intruded status, $F(1,94) = 11.83$, $MSE = 80.7$, $p < .05$. Participants who were intruded upon took longer to choose a video (15.1 min, $SD = 10.8$) than participants who were not intruded upon (8.7 min, $SD = 7.6$).

The interaction between actor type and intruded status was not significant, $F(1,94) = 1.38$, $MSE = 80.7$, $p = .24$. The mean video selection times for the four conditions are presented in Table C.7. For both main actors and intruders, there was an increase in selection time if they were intruded upon.

■ ■ ■ ■ ■ ■
References

Glenberg, A. M. (1996). *Learning from data: An introduction to statistical reasoning* (2nd Ed.). Mahwah, NJ: Erlbaum.

Rosnow, R. L., & Rosnow, M. (2001). *Writing papers in psychology: A student guide* (5th Ed.). Belmont, CA: Wadsworth.

Presenting Your Work

This appendix describes how you should present your work. Tips are provided to help you present your work as a poster or as an oral presentation. A sample poster and sample presentation are also included.

■ ■ ■ ■ ■ ■
Poster Presentations

Poster presentations are commonly used at research conferences because they provide a way for a lot of people to present their work simultaneously. For example, at the Psychonomic Society meetings in the fall of 1998, it took only four poster sessions to present 393 posters and two and a half days of concurrent talks to present 320 spoken presentations. A lot more people will have a chance to present if a poster format is used (Psychonomic Society Publications, 1998).

Poster presentations are also used because they allow for more interaction between the presenter and the audience. A poster will generally be seen by fewer people than may attend an oral presentation, but the people who see it will have an opportunity to discuss it with the presenter. The audience will also be composed primarily of people who are interested in hearing about the research being presented. Because of the opportunity for interaction, posters are frequently presented at undergraduate research conferences.

How Much Should Be Included?

When planning a poster presentation, you need to think about how the audience will view the poster. You will either tack individual panels to a wall board or glue them to a trifold presentation stand. If you are using a trifold stand, it will be placed on a table for presentation. You will stand near the poster to discuss it as people read it. If the poster is on a table with another poster, the scene can get very crowded. Here are some general design considerations to make it easier for the audience to see and understand the poster.

1. Do not try to fit every detail of the research onto the poster. Provide an adequate summary but try to limit how much time a person has to spend reading. If you are concerned about details, you can prepare a handout with more information that you can distribute to interested visitors.
2. Avoid pages with nothing but text in long paragraphs. A poster is not a paper, and people will not have much time to read.
3. Try not to use more than eight pieces of paper to present your poster. A good mix would be one for an abstract, one for an introduction, one for a method section, two for results (one text and one figure), and one for discussion. That will allow room for a large title and your name.

To reiterate, the purpose of the poster format is to allow you to discuss your work with the audience. Provide enough detail to let your visitors understand the experiment and plan to convey additional information in conversation.

How Should the Poster Be Presented?

You need to make your poster visually appealing. Gluing eight pieces of paper to a poster board and standing it on a table will be very boring. In the marketplace of a poster session, few people will be interested in seeing what you have to say. But you do not want to go too far with decorating your poster. Do not make it so cluttered that the research is obscured. Here are some tips that might help.

1. Arrange the information so that a person can read each column of the poster in one pass from left to right. If there is a crowd, people will not be able to move back and forth in front of the poster. One way to accomplish this is to arrange the information in columns instead of rows.
2. Make the print large enough to be read at a distance of at least three feet.
3. Be sure that the title can be read from an even greater distance than the rest of the poster. People will be looking for particular posters if there are time constraints. Help them find your poster if they are looking for it.
4. Use bullets and space out the information. Try to write in bite-sized chunks. This makes the poster easier to read at a distance.
5. Convey as much information as possible in figures and illustrations. Make sure these are also large enough to be read at a distance.
6. Glue each piece of paper to colored backing paper. My students usually use two colors. For example, you may use a bright blue and a bright yellow. The colors you choose should make the poster text stand out. Figure D.1 illustrates one arrangement of backing paper and text.
7. Apply some decoration to give the poster visual appeal. For example, one group of students conducted a memory study for real-world information. They asked people for memories from the movie *Titanic* and the movie *As Good as It Gets*. They proposed that the emotional content of *Titanic* would lead to more memories than *As Good as It Gets*. For the poster, the

Figure D.1 A sample poster and backing paper layout.

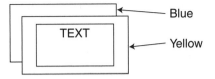

students downloaded pictures of the *Titanic* and the movie poster from *As Good as It Gets*, and they placed the pictures around the text panels.

8. You should dress up for the presentation.

A good rule of thumb is to try to imagine yourself as a member of the audience at a poster session. What would make you interested in reading a poster? How would you want the poster to be designed so that it was easy to understand?

A Sample Poster

An example of the amount of material that you will need to include is presented in Figure D.2. This poster was presented at the fall 1998 MTSU Psychology Day. The poster won a research prize in its category. Each section was presented on a separate piece of paper.

Note that this experiment won a research prize even though the hypothesis was not supported. You may be concerned about reporting research that did not work out, but those concerns are unfounded. Many experiments do not support the hypothesis; this is especially true of experiments conducted in research methods laboratory classes. You have a very limited amount of time to design the experiment, and you only get one chance to collect data. If the experiment was well designed, and if you present it well, your audience will still have an opportunity to learn something from your results.

Figure D.2 A sample poster presentation.
(Fox, Saulter, & Norman, 1998. Reprinted by permission.)

The Effect of Room Color on Mood

Tracey Fox, Patti Saulter, and Neil Norman

ABSTRACT

The question was Does the color of a room affect people's mood? Previous research results have been mixed, but blue tends to be calming and red tends to cause anxiety. We manipulated room color using colored lights in a white room. One group of participants was in a red room, the other was in a blue room. We measured mood by looking for Stroop interference for mood-congruent words. We found no main effect of room color for percent correct or reaction time on the Stroop task.

(continued on next page)

Figure D.2 A sample poster presentation *(continued)*.

INTRODUCTION

- How does the color of the environment influence mood? Jacobs & Suess (1975) found that manipulating room color using colored lights affected anxiety. Red and yellow lights produced more anxious moods than blue and green lights. However, research on this topic has been mixed. Some studies find no effect, others find the opposite effect. Our goal was to attempt to develop a more reliable dependent variable to see if we could clarify the relationship between room color and mood.

- Research has shown that Stroop interference occurs for words that match a person's psychological state. For example, Cooper and Todd (1997) found that anorexics have more interference for shape words (e.g. "thigh") than control words.

- Richards, French, Johnson, Naparstek, and Williams (1992) found more Stroop interference for anxiety words in people who score high on a trait anxiety scale.

- Our goal was to use a Stroop interference paradigm to measure anxiety after participants sat in a blue or red room.

METHOD

- There were 32 participants, 16 were in a blue room and 16 were in a red room.

- Room color was manipulated by placing gels over can lights in the room. We used 40 watt bulbs. The room was saturated with the light, but the overall lighting was dim.

- Participants started by sitting in the appropriately colored room for 10 minutes. To occupy their time, participants attempted to solve as many Tangram puzzles as possible. The puzzles were pictures of people that participants had to recreate using seven shapes.

- Participants then completed a Stroop interference task. They saw three sets of words, 48 in each set. The sets were randomly ordered for each participant. One set contained anxious words ("tense," "aroused," "excited," "hostile"). One set contained soothed words ("soothed," "relaxed," "serene," "peace"). The last set contained neutral words ("one," "two," "three," "four"). The words were red, green, yellow, or blue. The room for the Stroop test was white.

- We compared average response time and error rate for the three word types for people in the two room colors.

(continued on next page)

Figure D.2 A sample poster presentation *(continued)*.

RESULTS

- Data from the neutral words were not used in the analysis because participants did not differ on these words, and this condition did not differ from either of the other conditions.

- For the reaction times, there was no main effect for room color. The main effect for word type was significant. Tense words ($M = 831$ ms) were responded to more slowly than soothed words ($M = 780$ ms), $F(1,30) = 5.83$, $MSE = 7011.54$.

- We were expecting a room color X word type interaction. We expected participants in the blue room to take longer to respond to soothed words, and participants in the red room to take longer to respond to tense words. This effect was not significant. However, participants in the red room did take longer to name the colors of tense words than participants in the blue room. These data are illustrated in Figure 1.

- The results of the accuracy data were similar. There was no main effect for room color. Participants were marginally more accurate for tense words ($M = 96\%$) than for soothed words ($M = 95\%$), $F(1,30) = 3.00$, $MSE = .001$, p = .09. The interaction was not significant. The accuracy data were less meaningful due to a ceiling effect.

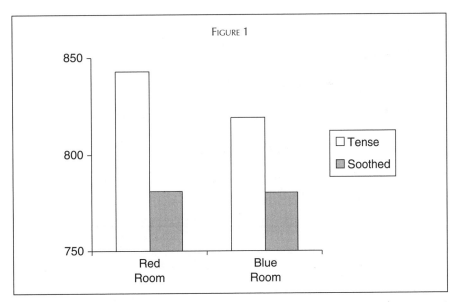

FIGURE 1

(continued on next page)

Figure D.2   A sample poster presentation *(continued)*.

DISCUSSION

- We did not find a difference in naming time for the colors of the words based on room color. It may be that there was no difference because room color has no effect on mood.

- However, a number of alternative explanations are also possible.
  (1) The Stroop test did not take place in the colored room. This might have reduced differences due to color.
  (2) The colors were not intense enough. The red gels were more intense than the blue gels. This meant the red room was more red than the blue room was blue. This lack of color may have reduced any differences.
  (3) The Tangram puzzles may have produced anxiety in all participants. Overall, the anxiety words took longer, regardless of condition.
  (4) Running participants in groups may have increased anxiety. Some participants reported being frustrated with their partners because they weren't allowed to use the puzzle.

- In conclusion, even though Stroop interference has been shown to be sensitive to changes in anxiety, we found no changes in Stroop interference based on the color of the room.

Oral Presentations

Oral presentations give researchers an opportunity to share their latest research with a large audience. An oral presentation is more formal than a poster presentation, and there is less opportunity for audience participation.

How Much Should Be Included?

Most of the suggestions for a poster presentation also apply to an oral presentation. Here are some tips:

1. Do not try to fit every detail of the research into the presentation. Provide an adequate summary, but remember the limitations of oral presentation formats. People will only be able to digest a certain amount of material in 10–15 minutes. If you stick too closely to details, the audience will lose the thread of the presentation.
2. Focus on questions. Pose a research question and answer it. Help the audience to understand your motivation for each part of the experiment. Why is this an interesting question? Why are you using this methodology to answer it? Why are the results important?
3. Use a lot of overheads or slides. Let the audience follow along the outline of the presentation as you go. Someone who temporarily loses track of the presentation can always catch up by looking at the overheads you provide.

4. A standard format is 15 minutes for each presenter. Plan for 12 minutes of presentation and three minutes of questions. In your 12 minutes, spend around four setting up the problem, two discussing the methodology, two discussing results, and four for the discussion.

How Should the Talk Be Presented?

You have sat through boring presentations. You have also seen interesting presentations. Avoid the characteristics of boring presentations and copy the characteristics of interesting presentations. You can deliver a professional presentation and still be a stimulating speaker. Here are some tips that may help:

1. Memorize the beginning of the presentation word for word. A good opening is to read your title and mention all of the people who participated in the project. This will get you started and help with the initial nervousness.
2. Do not read your talk. You will bore your audience, and you will make it impossible for them to pay attention. Instead, use overheads as a memory cue and speak spontaneously. For example, you may put the number of participants on an overhead. This will remind you to mention the number of participants, and give you an opportunity to describe them in detail.
3. Do have notes prepared for each section. You may panic and be unable to remember what you wanted to say. If you have notes, you can use them for backup. You can consult your notes without reading them to the audience. It is acceptable to pause between sentences and think about what you want to say next.
4. Speak slowly enough that the audience can follow your ideas, but do not talk in a monotone.
5. Anything you show on the overhead projector should be printed neatly in large, bold type. There is nothing more frustrating than struggling to read the overheads during a presentation.
6. Keep your visual aids simple. The audience has a limited amount of time to read and understand them. If everyone is struggling to understand what is on the overhead projector, nobody will be listening to you.
7. Never present a page full of statistics or text and tell the audience to read it for themselves. If it is important for the audience to read something, read it to them. If doing this makes you feel as though you are spending too much time reading to the audience, you are. Cut back the amount of material that you are presenting.
8. Do not assume that the audience will be able to see something just because you put it on the overhead projector. There may be obstructions, or it may be hard to see from the back of the room. Always describe what you are presenting.
9. Do not hover around the overhead projector. Never point to anything on the projector, point to the screen. Standing by the projector is likely to block the audience's view.
10. Feel free to move around, but do not move so much that you distract the audience.

11. Rehearse the whole presentation at least once, and try to rehearse in front of an audience. Let the test audience help you decide if the talk is clear.
12. Dress up for the presentation.

You will probably be nervous before the presentation. Here are some tips to help settle your nerves:

1. Rehearse thoroughly. If you know what you want to say, you will feel better about saying it.
2. Get the audience to do something. This will distract them temporarily, and it will put you in control of the room. For example, one presenter I saw surveyed the audience to see if they believed various "facts" (e.g., you will do better on a multiple choice exam if you do not change your answers). After getting the audience to express an opinion, he pointed out that the "facts" were all wrong. The audience was then very eager to hear why the facts were wrong, and the speaker got a moment at the beginning of his talk to take a deep breath and let the audience do some of the work. Another nice feature of this presentation was that the audience was embarrassed for expressing belief in ideas that were false. The awkwardness shifted from the speaker to the audience.
3. An interested audience is easier to talk to than a bored audience. Get the audience interested by giving them something to do (as above). You can also make a provocative statement. I once saw a presenter who started by saying that there was no such thing as memory. Then he set out to prove it by giving the audience a memory demonstration. That combined two elements to build interest, and the audience was very involved by the time he got down to the main part of the talk.
4. Keep these things in mind:
    a. Fifteen minutes goes by very quickly when you are speaking.
    b. Nobody will try to ask you a question that you cannot answer.
    c. If you do not know the answer to someone's question, you can say, "I don't know." You can also try to involve the person asking the question in speculating about the answer.
    d. You can direct the audience's questions to topics you know. For example, you might say, "The exact details of this procedure are not essential, but if you would like to know them, we can discuss it in the question period." Try not to do this too much because it can be annoying.

A Sample Presentation

Given the rules above, it is not possible to show you a sample talk. I have never written a talk in my life, and I would not want you to write a talk either. If I were going to present the room color experiment in the poster above, I would make notes similar to the poster. Then I would memorize most of the information on the notes and prepare a series of overheads to help me remember what I wanted to say. Sample overheads from this talk are presented in Figure D.3.

Figure D.3 Sample oral presentation overheads.

INTRODUCTION

- How does the color of the environment influence mood?
  Jacobs & Suess (1975)
  Other studies

- Stroop interference occurs for words that match a person's psychological state.
  Cooper and Todd (1997)
  Richards, French, Johnson, Naparstek, and Williams (1992)

- Our goal was to use a Stroop interference paradigm to measure anxiety after participants sat in a blue or red room.

METHOD

- 32 participants, 16 in a blue room and 16 in a red room.

- Participants sat in the appropriately colored room for 10 minutes completing Tangram puzzles.

  [I would show some Tangram puzzles here, and ask the audience to solve the puzzles. I would pick one easy puzzle and one hard puzzle to let the audience get some idea of the task.]

- Stroop interference task.

RESULTS

- No main effect for room color.

- Main effect for word type.
  Tense words $M = 831$ ms
  Soothed words $M = 780$ ms [The statistics would be in a smaller font size.]
  $F(1,30) = 5.83$

- No room color × word type interaction.

  [I would show Figure 1 here.]

DISCUSSION

- The hypothesis was not supported.

- Possible explanations:
  1. The Stroop test did not take place in the colored room.
  2. The colors were not intense enough.
  3. The Tangram puzzles may have produced anxiety in all participants.
  4. Running participants in groups may have increased anxiety.

- In conclusion, we found no changes in Stroop interference based on the color of the room.

Obviously, the overheads do not contain enough information to fully understand the experiment. I would flesh them out with the talk. For the opening, I would find a provocative statement in the literature or find an anecdote about room color and mood. For example, statistics on how the environment influences productivity would help motivate the audience to be interested in my research; or an anecdote about putting prisoners in pink holding cells may be good for a laugh.

I would bring to the presentation my overheads, plus cards with the detailed information to flesh out the talk. I do not usually rely on the cards, but they are nice when you forget what you want to say. I would also bring additional information that I did not plan to present. I like to be prepared in case someone asks a question that I did not anticipate. Again, feeling prepared makes you less nervous.

■ ■ ■ ■ ■ ■
References

Fox, T., Saulter, P., & Norman, N. (1998, November). *The Effect of Room Color on Mood.* Poster presented at the Middle Tennessee State University Psychology Day, Murfreesboro, TN. Used with permission of the author.

Psychonomic Society Publications. (1998). *Abstracts of the Psychonomic Society, 3.*

Installing the Software

This appendix describes how to install the software from the CD-ROM.

■ ■ ■ ■ ■ ■
Macintosh Users

Installing the Software

Copy the program you want to use from the CD-ROM to your desktop. Use the following steps:

1. Open the CD-ROM.
2. Select the program or folder you wish to copy and drag it to your hard drive. (For software in a folder, be sure to install the entire folder, not just the program.)
3. Open the hard drive.
4. Select the program or folder and drag it to the desktop.

For all of the software, all of the stimulus paths in the "Experiments" folders are "hard" coded. This means that the software on your computer must be located in the same place as the software on the source computer. When I set the paths, the software folders were on my desktop, and all of the stimulus folders were in the software folders. If you choose not to leave the software on your desktop, you will need to open the parameter sets that you want to run and reset the stimulus paths. To do this, use the software to open any stimulus file after the software is in its final location. To run your parameter sets on multiple computers, be sure that the software folder and stimuli are in the same place on all of the computers. I suggest that you *do not* rearrange the stimulus folders within the software folder.

Features

The following features have been tested:

1. The software will work with both the OnGuard™ and At Ease™ security systems. However, you will need an administrator password to place the software on the machine. If you set the correct permissions, you will be able to collect data while the security software is running.
2. The software does not conflict with Virex™ antivirus protection.
3. As long as all data files are saved in the main folder, the software is very easy to uninstall (by dragging the software folder to the trash).

Problems

Known bugs, conflicts, and limitations include:

1. If you run some versions of Netscape™ before collecting reaction times, the computer will not wait for a key-press before continuing. Always restart your computer after running Netscape before collecting data.
2. You must be running at least System 7. The software has been tested in System 7.5 and System 8. The software has not been tested for System 9.0 or OS X.

■ ■ ■ ■ ■ ■
Windows Users

Installing the Software

Use the installers on the CD-ROM to install the software. Use the following steps:

1. Double-click the installer for the software you want to install.
2. Follow the instructions on screen.
3. Be sure to run the installer for the accompanying analysis software. After each installation, you will be asked to restart your computer. If you know you will be installing an analysis program, you can skip the restart for the experiment program, install the analysis program, and then restart. On some versions of Windows 98, when doing more than one install without restarting, you may need to double-click the second installer twice to get it to run.

Software icons will be placed in Start | Programs | RM Laboratory Manual. The software folder will be on your hard drive in C:\Program Files\RM Laboratory Manual. All of the stimulus materials you need will be in the software folder. (If your directory structure is nonstandard, the final location may be slightly different.)

For all of the software, all of the stimulus paths in the "Experiments" folders are "hard" coded. This means that the software on your computer must be located in the same place as the software on the source computer. When I set the paths, the software folders were in C:\Program Files\RM Laboratory Manual. If you choose not to leave the software in the default location, you will need to open the parameter sets that you want to run and reset the stimulus paths. To do this, use the software to open any stimulus file after the software is in its final location. To run your parameter sets on multiple computers, be sure that the software folder and stimuli are in the same place on all of the computers. I suggest that you *do not* rearrange the stimulus folders within the software folder, and that you *do* leave the software folder in its default location.

Features

The following features have been tested:

1. The software will work with the Fortress™ security system. However, you will need an administrator password to place the software on the machine. If you set the correct permissions, you will be able to collect data while the security software is running.
2. The software does not conflict with FProt™ antivirus protection.
3. The software offers easy uninstallation for systems managers (using the "Add/Remove Programs" Control Panel).
4. The software has been tested for Windows 95 and Windows 98. The software has not been tested in Windows 3.x or Windows 2000. It should run in Windows 2000; it may not work in Windows 3.x.

Problems

Known bugs, conflicts, and limitations include:

1. All timing is done with the Windows timer. Depending on the experiment, that can introduce some variability into the results. Always quit all other programs before collecting reaction time data.
2. When running from stimuli stored on a floppy, the software will pause while the floppy is being accessed. This may affect timing, and it will definitely be noticeable for participants.

Index

Boldface page numbers in the index indicate pages where the term is defined.